Gooseberry Patch Co.®

A Country Store In Your Mailbox®

ALMOST
♥
Homemade

Gooseberry Patch

A Country Store In Your Mailbox®

Gooseberry Patch
600 London Road
P.O. Box 190
Delaware, OH 43015

www.gooseberrypatch.com
1·800·854·6673

Copyright 2005, Gooseberry Patch 1-931890-74-9
Second Printing, February, 2006

Do you have a tried & true recipe...

tip, craft or memory that you'd like to see featured in a **Gooseberry
Patch** book? Visit our website at **www.gooseberrypatch.com**, register
and follow the easy steps to submit your favorite family recipe.
Or send them to us at:

Gooseberry Patch
Attn: Book Dept.
P.O. Box 190
Delaware, OH 43015

Don't forget to include the number of servings your recipe makes,
plus your name, street address, phone number and e-mail address.
If we select your recipe, your name will appear right along with
it...and you'll receive a **FREE** copy of the book!

Contents

Dedication

To everyone who knows
the secret ingredient of every
home-cooked meal is love!

Appreciation

To all of our **Gooseberry Patch** family
who generously shared tried & true
recipes with us...thanks!

Blissful Breakfasts

Rise & Shine Quiche

Marsha Bishoff
Washington, IL

I love this combination of potatoes, eggs and ham!
It's tasty made with bacon and a little chopped onion too.

24-oz. pkg. frozen diced
   potatoes, thawed
1/3 c. butter, melted
1 c. shredded Cheddar cheese
1 c. shredded Swiss cheese

1 c. cooked ham, diced
1/2 c. milk
2 eggs
1/4 t. seasoned salt

Press potatoes into the bottom of a greased 9"x9" baking pan; brush with butter. Bake at 425 degrees for 25 minutes; top with cheeses and ham. Set aside. Beat milk, eggs and salt; pour over cheese mixture. Reduce heat to 350 degrees and bake for 30 to 40 minutes. Serves 6.

Get the day off to a great start...put together a Rise & Shine Quiche or a breakfast casserole and refrigerate. The next day, pop it in the oven for a hot, hearty breakfast with no fuss at all!

Blissful Breakfasts

Bacon & Egg Tarts

Virginia Watson
Scranton, PA

An elegant dish for a special breakfast.

11-oz. pkg. pie crust mix
6-oz. pkg. sliced Canadian
   bacon
1 c. shredded Cheddar cheese,
   divided

4 eggs
1/4 c. milk, divided
nutmeg and pepper to taste

Prepare pastry dough for one pie crust as directed on package; divide into 4 equal parts. Roll each part into a 6-inch circle on a floured surface. Press circles into 4 ungreased 3"x2" muffin cups and bake at 425 degrees for 8 to 10 minutes, until golden. Cool for 5 minutes in cups; remove to an ungreased baking sheet. Place 2 slices bacon in the bottom of each pastry cup; sprinkle each with 1/4 cup cheese. Place one egg in each cup; top each with one tablespoon milk. Sprinkle with nutmeg and pepper. Reduce oven to 350 degrees and bake for 15 to 20 minutes, until eggs are soft-cooked. Makes 4 tarts.

Add whimsy to your breakfast table with vintage salt & pepper shakers in fun shapes. Look for 'em at yard sales or bring your grandmother's old shakers out of the cupboard!

Cream Cheesy Strudel

Donna Simonson
Sullivan, OH

*Sprinkle with colored sugar in holiday colors...red and green
for Christmas, yellow and pink for Easter.*

2 8-oz. tubes refrigerated
   crescent rolls, divided
2 8-oz. pkgs. cream cheese,
   softened

1 egg
1/2 c. plus 2 T. sugar, divided
1 t. vanilla extract
1/4 t. cinnamon

Arrange one tube crescent rolls in the bottom of an ungreased
13"x9" baking pan. Mix cream cheese, egg, 1/2 cup sugar and
vanilla; spread over crescent rolls. Cover with remaining crescent rolls;
sprinkle with cinnamon and remaining sugar. Bake at 375 degrees for
11 to 13 minutes. Cut into squares to serve. Makes 1-1/2 to 2 dozen.

A recipe for success! Always check the recipe and make sure
you have everything on hand before you start...no quick trips
to the store for a forgotten ingredient.

Blissful Breakfasts

Blueberry Puffs

Kathy Grashoff
Fort Wayne, IN

*The aroma of home-baked blueberry goodness will bring
your sleepy family right to the kitchen!*

1 c. buttermilk biscuit baking
   mix
1 c. multi-grain pancake mix
2 eggs, beaten

2/3 c. milk
1/3 c. sugar
2 T. butter, melted
1 c. blueberries

Combine the 2 mixes; set aside. Mix eggs, milk, sugar and butter
together; add to dry mixes. Fold in blueberries; fill greased muffin
cups 3/4 full. Bake at 400 degrees for 15 to 20 minutes; remove to
a wire rack to cool. Makes one dozen.

Use an old-fashioned ice cream scoop to fill muffin cups
with batter...no spills, no drips and the muffins
turn out perfectly sized!

Farmers' Breakfast Casserole

Laurie Anderson
Columbia, TN

*A complete, extra-hearty breakfast...simply add a
fresh fruit cup and a hot beverage.*

3 c. frozen shredded
  hashbrowns
1 c. shredded Cheddar or
  Monterey Jack cheese
1 c. cooked ham or bacon, diced

1/4 c. green onion, diced
4 eggs, beaten
12-oz. can evaporated milk
1/4 t. pepper
1/8 t. salt

Arrange hashbrowns evenly in the bottom of a greased 13"x9" baking
pan. Sprinkle with cheese, ham or bacon and onion; set aside.
Combine eggs, milk, pepper and salt in a mixing bowl; blend well.
Pour egg mixture over potato mixture; cover and refrigerate for
several hours or overnight. Bake, uncovered, at 350 degrees until
center is set, 40 to 45 minutes if chilled several hours or 55 to
60 minutes if chilled overnight. Makes 6 to 8 servings.

Egg dishes are a perfect way to use up tasty tidbits
from the fridge...ham, deli meats, chopped veggies and
cheese. Warm briefly in a skillet and set aside for an
omelet filling or scramble the eggs right in.

Blissful Breakfasts

Breakfast Pizza

Francie Stutzman
Dalton, OH

Kids will love this...perfect for waking up slumber party guests!

8-oz. tube refrigerated
  crescent rolls
1 lb. ground sausage, browned
  and drained
1 c. frozen diced potatoes,
  thawed

1 c. shredded Cheddar cheese
5 eggs
1/4 c. milk
1/2 t. salt
1/8 t. pepper
2 T. grated Parmesan cheese

Separate crescent rolls into 8 triangles. Arrange rolls with points
toward center in an ungreased 12" pizza pan. Press over bottom and
up sides to form crust; seal perforations. Spoon browned sausage over
crust. Sprinkle with potatoes; top with Cheddar cheese. Set aside. In a
bowl, beat together eggs, milk, salt and pepper. Pour over crust.
Sprinkle Parmesan cheese over the top. Bake at 375 degrees for
25 to 30 minutes. Cut into wedges to serve. Makes 6 servings.

Greet the day with a bright blossom at each place setting.
Tiny containers like egg cups, toothpick holders and
cream pitchers make charming little vases.

Wake-Up Fruit Salad

Marian Buckley
Fontana, CA

Add a sprinkle of granola for a crunchy topping.

26-oz. jar mixed fruit, drained
2 bananas, sliced
1 c. blueberries

1/2 c. celery, sliced
1/4 to 1/2 c. poppy seed
   salad dressing

Combine mixed fruit, bananas, blueberries and celery in a bowl. Toss with dressing. Serves 6 to 8.

Break-of-Day Smoothie

Cheri Maxwell
Gulf Breeze, FL

Make this just the way you like it, using your favorite flavors of yogurt and fruit juice.

15-1/4 oz. can fruit cocktail
8-oz. container vanilla yogurt
1 c. pineapple juice

6 to 8 ice cubes
Optional: 3 to 4 T. wheat germ

Combine all ingredients in a blender. Blend until smooth. Serves 2.

Serve fruit for breakfast in pretty sundae dishes...top with a dollop of yogurt or even whipped topping for a sweet treat that's good for you!

Blissful Breakfasts

Creamy Fruit Cocktail Salad

Mary Murray
Gooseberry Patch

Drizzle the rest of the condensed milk over hot oatmeal
for a sweet treat!

2 8-oz. pkgs. cream cheese,
   softened
3/4 to 1 c. sweetened
   condensed milk

2 15-1/4 oz. cans fruit cocktail,
   drained and juice reserved
3 T. maraschino cherries, halved
1 banana, sliced

Combine cream cheese and condensed milk in a bowl; blend with an electric mixer on medium speed until smooth. Add reserved fruit cocktail juice; blend well. Fold in remaining ingredients with a spoon; stir to coat. Cover and chill for 30 minutes. Serves 8.

Did you know...eggs that have been refrigerated
for 7 to 10 days usually peel much more easily
when hard-boiled than fresh eggs.

Banana Nut Bread

Beth Goblirsch
Minneapolis, MN

Wrap in a pretty tea towel for a quick gift.

1 c. sugar
8-oz. pkg. cream cheese,
  softened
1 c. bananas, mashed

2 eggs
2 c. biscuit baking mix
1/2 c. chopped pecans

Blend sugar and cream cheese; beat in bananas and eggs. Add baking mix and pecans; stir until moistened. Pour into a greased 9"x5" loaf pan; bake at 350 degrees for one hour. Cool before slicing. Makes 10 to 12 servings.

Maple-Raisin-Walnut Spread

Cora Baker
La Rue, OH

I love to spread this flavorful cream cheese on warm toasted bagels.

8-oz. pkg. cream cheese,
  softened
1 T. chopped walnuts
1 T. raisins
1 t. water

3-1/2 T. dark brown sugar,
  packed
1/8 t. maple extract
1/8 t. cinnamon

Whip cream cheese until smooth; set aside. Grind walnuts coarsely in a food processor or blender; set aside. Place raisins and water in food processor; chop into small pieces. Combine raisin mixture and one teaspoon walnuts with cream cheese; mix well. Add remaining walnuts, sugar, extract and cinnamon; mix well, cover and chill until firm. Makes 1-1/4 cups.

Gooey Coffee Cake

Lee McDougal
Alpine, CA

Oh boy, we can't wait for it to cool!

18-1/2 oz. pkg. yellow cake mix
3 eggs, divided and beaten
1/2 c. butter, softened
8-oz. pkg. cream cheese,
    softened

3-3/4 c. powdered sugar
1 t. vanilla extract
Garnish: sliced almonds

Combine cake mix, one egg and butter; pat into the bottom of a lightly greased 13"x9" baking pan. Set aside. Mix remaining eggs, cream cheese, sugar and vanilla together; pour over cake mixture. Top with almonds; bake at 350 degrees for 25 minutes. Cool; cut into squares. Serves 12.

Liven up plain orange juice with a splash of sparkling white grape juice or ginger ale...serve in stemmed glasses for a festive breakfast beverage.

Cheesy Scramblin' Pizza

Dianne Gregory
Sheridan, AR

With ready-to-use pizza crust and bacon slices,
this is as easy to make as it is tasty.

6 eggs
1/4 c. milk
1/4 c. green onion, sliced
1 tomato, chopped
12-inch Italian pizza crust

8-oz. pkg. pasteurized
   processed cheese spread,
   cubed
6 slices bacon, crisply cooked
   and cut into 1-inch pieces

Whisk together eggs, milk, onion and tomato in a medium bowl; pour into a non-stick skillet sprayed with non-stick vegetable spray. Cook on medium-low heat until eggs are set, stirring occasionally. Set aside. Place pizza crust on an ungreased baking sheet. Top with egg mixture and cheese; sprinkle with bacon. Bake at 450 degrees for 10 minutes, or until cheese is melted. Cut into wedges to serve. Makes 6 to 8 servings.

Bacon is so tasty, but can be messy to fry...bake it instead!
Lay bacon slices on a jelly-roll pan and bake at 350 degrees
for 15 to 20 minutes, until it's as crisp as you like.
Drain well on paper towels.

Blissful Breakfasts

Make-Ahead Breakfast Casserole

Valarie Dennard
Palatka, FL

I prepare this casserole for Sunday School class breakfasts and for our family's annual Christmas breakfast. There are never any leftovers!

2-1/2 c. seasoned croutons
1 lb. ground spicy pork sausage, browned and drained
4 eggs
2-1/4 c. milk
10-3/4 oz. can cream of mushroom soup
4-1/2 oz. can mushrooms, drained and chopped

10-oz. pkg. frozen chopped spinach, thawed and well drained
1 c. shredded sharp Cheddar cheese
1 c. shredded Monterey Jack cheese
1/4 t. dry mustard

Spread croutons in a greased 13"x9" baking pan; top with sausage and set aside. Whisk together eggs and milk in a large bowl until well blended. Stir in remaining ingredients. Pour egg mixture over sausage and croutons; cover and refrigerate overnight. Bake at 325 degrees for 50 to 55 minutes, until set and golden on top. Makes 6 to 8 servings.

Egg dishes have a kind of elegance, a freshness, an allure which sets them quite apart from any other kind of food.

-Elizabeth David

Ham & Cheese Muffins

Leanne Wheless
Borger, TX

A tasty portable breakfast...just the thing when you're hurrying out the door!

1 T. butter
1/3 c. dried, minced onion
8-oz. pkg. shredded Cheddar
    cheese
1-1/2 c. biscuit baking mix

1/2 c. milk
2 eggs
1 c. cooked ham, finely chopped
1 t. hickory smoked salt

Melt butter in a skillet. Add onion and cook over low heat until softened; set aside. Combine cheese and biscuit mix in a bowl; stir in milk and eggs just until moistened. Fold in ham, softened onion and salt. Fill 12 greased muffin cups 3/4 full. Bake at 425 degrees for 13 to 15 minutes, or until a toothpick comes out clean. Let cool for 5 minutes before removing from muffin cups. Serve warm. Makes one dozen.

A slick trick when baking muffins! Grease muffin cups on the bottoms and just halfway up the sides...muffins will bake up nicely domed on top.

Blissful Breakfasts

Praline Pecan Biscuits

Debra Eaton
Mesa, AZ

Serve warm with honey...so good!

36 pecan halves
1/2 c. butter, sliced
1/2 c. brown sugar, packed
1 T. cinnamon

2 c. buttermilk biscuit
   baking mix
1/3 c. milk
1/3 c. applesauce

In each cup of a greased 12-cup muffin tin, place 3 pecan halves, 2 teaspoons butter and 2 teaspoons brown sugar. Bake at 450 degrees just until butter melts; set aside. Combine remaining ingredients in a mixing bowl, beating about 20 strokes. Spoon mixture into muffin cups. Bake for 10 minutes at 450 degrees; invert on a serving plate. Serve warm. Makes one dozen.

Serve up special coffee with breakfast...add a dash
of nutmeg, cinnamon or orange zest just before brewing.
A drop of vanilla added at serving time is nice too.

Yummy Apple-Cinnamon Ring

Teresa Smith
Wellston, OK

Smells almost as delightful as it tastes!

3 8-oz. tubes refrigerated
   biscuits, quartered
1 c. sugar
1 T. cinnamon

2 apples, cored, peeled
   and chopped
1/2 c. chopped pecans
1/2 c. butter, melted

Toss quartered biscuits with remaining ingredients except for butter; fill a greased and floured Bundt® pan with biscuit mixture. Pour butter over top. Bake at 375 degrees for 25 to 30 minutes. Let cool for 5 minutes; invert onto a serving platter. Makes 10 to 12 servings.

No tube pan on hand? Try setting a clean, tin soup can in the center of a deep cake pan. Grease and flour both before adding ingredients...it works great!

Blissful Breakfasts

Salsa & Hashbrown Skillet

Lynda McCormick
Burkburnett, TX

Top with a dollop of sour cream.

1/4 c. butter
3 c. frozen shredded
   hashbrowns with peppers
   and onions, thawed

2 eggs, beaten
1 c. shredded sharp Cheddar
   cheese
1/2 c. chunky salsa, drained

Melt butter in a skillet over medium heat. Add hashbrowns; cook for 5 minutes. Pour eggs over top; reduce heat and cook for 5 minutes, or until eggs are set. Flip over; sprinkle with cheese and heat until cheese melts. Serve with salsa. Serves 4.

Scramblin' Asparagus-Potato Eggs

Melanie Lowe
Dover, DE

Quick & easy with canned veggies...a great way to use leftovers too! Substitute about 1-1/2 cups each of fresh asparagus and potatoes.

2 t. oil
1 c. onion, chopped
1/2 t. dried basil
1 c. cooked ham, diced
14-1/2 oz. can new potatoes,
   drained and chopped

15-oz. can asparagus
   spears, drained
1 c. shredded Swiss cheese
4 eggs
1/4 c. water

Heat oil in a skillet over medium heat; sauté onion and basil until onion is tender. Add ham and potatoes; cook for 2 minutes. Arrange asparagus on top and sprinkle with cheese. Beat together eggs and water; pour over cheese. Cover and cook over low heat for 6 minutes. Uncover and cook an additional 5 minutes, or until set. Cut into wedges. Serves 6.

Lone Star Breakfast Casserole

Suzanne Fritz
Round Rock, TX

Satisfies Texas-size appetites!

8-oz. tube refrigerated
   crescent rolls
1 lb. ground sausage, browned
   and drained
1 c. mushrooms, sliced

12-oz. pkg. shredded Monterey
   Jack cheese, divided
6 eggs, beaten
10-3/4 oz. can cream of
   onion soup

Arrange rolls in the bottom of an ungreased 13"x9" baking pan; cover with sausage, mushrooms and half of the cheese. Set aside. Mix eggs and soup; pour over cheese. Sprinkle with remaining cheese; bake at 350 degrees for one hour. Serves 8.

Breakfast foods are so warm and comforting...try 'em for dinner as a special treat!

Blissful Breakfasts

Spinach-Cheddar Quiche

*Rita Silverman
Cheektowaga, NY*

*I like to create other delicious combinations using
a variety of cheeses and chopped vegetables.*

10-oz. pkg. frozen chopped
   spinach
1 T. butter
3 T. all-purpose flour
1 c. shredded Cheddar cheese

1 c. shredded mozzarella cheese
2 eggs
1 c. milk
9-inch pie crust

Cook spinach according to package directions; drain well. Add butter, flour and cheeses; mix well. Blend eggs and milk together; add to spinach mixture. Pour into pie crust; bake at 350 degrees for one hour. Serves 6 to 8.

Make a quick & easy savory crumb crust...so tasty for quiche.
Spread 2-1/2 tablespoons softened butter in a pie plate,
then firmly press 2-1/2 cups seasoned dry bread crumbs
or cracker crumbs into the butter. Freeze until firm,
pour in filling and bake as directed.

Green Chile Breakfast Bake

Maureen Miksis
Schaumburg, IL

Add a dash of hot pepper sauce if you like it spicy!

2 c. milk
4 eggs
1 c. biscuit baking mix
2 c. shredded Cheddar cheese
2 c. cooked ham, cubed

1/2 c. diced green chiles
32-oz. pkg. frozen hashbrown
    patties
salt and pepper to taste

Combine milk, eggs and baking mix; stir in cheese, ham and chiles.
Set aside. Arrange hashbrown patties in the bottom of a greased
13"x9" baking pan; pour egg mixture over the top. Sprinkle with
salt and pepper; bake at 400 degrees for 45 to 50 minutes. Let stand
5 minutes. Serves 6 to 8.

Are family members on different schedules?
Divide the ingredients for a breakfast casserole among
individual ramekins and bake as needed.

Blissful Breakfasts

Bette's Pecan Rolls

Michelle Campen
Peoria, IL

Sweet and tasty...easy to make for brunch.

1 c. chopped pecans
cinnamon to taste
2 loaves frozen bread dough,
    thawed
5-1/4 oz. pkg. cook & serve
    vanilla pudding mix

2 T. milk
1/2 c. butter, melted
1 c. brown sugar, packed

Sprinkle pecans in the bottom of a greased 13"x9" pan; sprinkle with cinnamon. Set aside. Tear dough into 24 walnut-size balls; arrange on top of pecans and set aside. Stir together pudding mix, milk, butter and sugar in a saucepan over low heat until melted; pour over rolls. Cover and refrigerate overnight. Bake at 350 degrees for 30 minutes; invert onto aluminum foil. Makes 2 dozen.

Butter-flavored non-stick vegetable spray is especially handy at breakfast time...use it to spray a skillet for cooking eggs, a waffle iron, pancake griddle or baking pan.

Monkey Bread

Diane Stansfield
Lancaster, CA

*No one can resist this pull-apart bread! Drizzle with warm
cream cheese frosting for an extra-special treat.*

4 12-oz. tubes refrigerated
   buttermilk biscuits
1-1/2 c. sugar, divided

2 t. cinnamon, divided
1/2 c. margarine, melted

Cut biscuits into quarters. Combine 3/4 cup sugar and one teaspoon
cinnamon in a small bowl; roll biscuits in mixture. Layer in a greased
Bundt® pan; set aside. Melt margarine in a small saucepan. Stir in
remaining sugar and cinnamon; pour over biscuits. Bake at
350 degrees for 40 minutes; let stand 3 to 5 minutes. Makes 12 to
15 servings.

Sweet cider-glazed sausages are a treat at breakfast.
Brown 1/2 pound breakfast sausages in a skillet and drain.
Add a cup of apple cider and simmer for about 10 minutes.

Blissful Breakfasts

Sausage Gravy & Biscuits

Sherry Gordon
Arlington Heights, IL

Hearty and filling...so good on a cold day!

1 lb. ground country sausage
2 T. margarine
1/4 c. all-purpose flour
4 c. milk

salt and pepper to taste
10-oz. tube refrigerated biscuits,
  baked and split

Brown sausage in a large skillet over medium heat. Stir in margarine until well blended; add flour and stir until mixture is thick. Reduce heat to medium-low and slowly add milk, stirring constantly, until mixture is thick and bubbly. Sprinkle with salt and pepper. Serve over warm biscuits. Serves 4.

Use a slow cooker set on low to keep sausage gravy,
scrambled eggs or other breakfast foods
warm and toasty for brunch.

South-of-the-Border Breakfast

Vickie

*We love to serve this hearty, spicy dish when having
special friends over for brunch.*

10 eggs
1 t. dried thyme
salt and pepper to taste
7-1/2 oz. pkg. corn tortillas
8-oz. pkg. shredded Cheddar
   cheese, divided
10-oz. can Mexican-style
   tomatoes with chiles, divided

1 lb. ground mild sausage,
   browned and drained
4-oz. can chopped green chiles
Optional: chopped jalapeños
   to taste
Optional: tortilla chips,
   sour cream, guacamole

Beat eggs with thyme, salt and pepper; set aside. Layer tortillas, one
cup cheese, half the tomatoes, sausage, chiles, jalapeños if using,
egg mixture, remaining cheese and tomatoes in a greased 2-quart
casserole dish. Bake at 350 degrees for 30 minutes, until eggs are set.
Top with crushed tortilla chips, sour cream and guacamole, if desired.
Serves 4 to 6.

Any egg dish turns into a portable breakfast when spooned
into a pita or rolled up in a tortilla!

Blissful Breakfasts

Blackberry Breakfast Cobbler

Carol Hickman
Kingsport, TN

So yummy, yet unbelievably easy!

1 T. cornstarch
15-oz. can blackberries, drained
   and juice reserved
1 t. lemon juice

8-oz. tube refrigerated
   cinnamon rolls
Garnish: frozen whipped
   topping, thawed

In a mixing bowl, dissolve cornstarch in reserved juice; add berries
and lemon juice. Mix well; spoon into a greased 8"x8" baking pan.
Set aside. Separate cinnamon rolls; arrange over blackberry mixture.
Bake at 400 degrees for 15 to 20 minutes, until golden and sauce is
bubbly. Garnish with a dollop of whipped topping. Serves 8.

All happiness depends on a leisurely breakfast.

–John Gunther

Pumpkin Coffee Cake

Gail Hageman
Albion, ME

A co-worker gave me this recipe. It's always a hit at potlucks!

2 16-oz. pkgs. pound cake mix
4 t. pumpkin pie spice
2 t. baking soda
3/4 c. water
15-oz. can pumpkin

4 eggs, beaten
3/4 c. brown sugar, packed
3/4 c. chopped walnuts
1/2 c. all-purpose flour
1/3 c. butter

Combine cake mix, pumpkin pie spice and baking soda; add water, pumpkin and eggs. Set aside. Blend brown sugar, walnuts, flour and butter until crumbly; set aside. Pour half of pumpkin mixture into a greased 13"x9" pan; sprinkle with half of the nut mixture. Pour on remaining pumpkin mixture; top with remaining nut mixture. Bake at 325 degrees for 50 minutes. Serves 8 to 10.

Set the breakfast table the night before...enjoy a relaxed breakfast in the morning!

Blissful Breakfasts

Graham-Streusel Coffee Cake

Dawn Webster
Elkhorn, WI

*This recipe is a family favorite! I like to make
these coffee cakes for holiday brunches.*

1-1/2 c. graham crackers,
   crushed
3/4 c. chopped walnuts
3/4 c. brown sugar, packed
1-1/2 t. cinnamon

2/3 c. margarine, melted
18-1/2 oz. pkg. yellow cake mix
1 c. water
1/4 c. oil
3 eggs

Combine crumbs, walnuts, brown sugar and cinnamon; stir in margarine. Set aside. Stir cake mix, water, oil and eggs together; beat for 1-1/2 minutes. Pour half of mixture into a greased 13"x9" baking pan; sprinkle with half the crumb mixture. Spoon remaining cake mixture over the top. sprinkle with remaining crumb mixture. Bake at 350 degrees for 35 to 40 minutes; cool. Drizzle Powdered Sugar Icing over the top. Serves 12 to 16.

Powdered Sugar Icing:

1 c. powdered sugar
1 t. vanilla extract

2 to 4 T. water

Mix sugar, vanilla and enough water to make a drizzling consistency.

Easy-squeezy! Place icing ingredients in a plastic zipping bag.
Squeeze to mix well, then snip off a small corner and squeeze
to drizzle over baked goods...just toss away the empty bag.

Williamsburg Bread

Lori Ginther
Beverly, OH

Whenever I take this recipe anywhere, I never bring any home!

2 8-oz. tubes refrigerated
   crescent rolls, divided
2 8-oz. pkgs. cream cheese,
   softened

1-1/2 c. sugar, divided
1 egg yolk
1 t. vanilla extract
2 t. cinnamon

Arrange one tube of crescent rolls in the bottom of a 13"x9" baking pan sprayed with non-stick vegetable spray; set aside. Mix together cream cheese, one cup sugar, egg yolk and vanilla; spread over rolls. Arrange remaining tube of rolls on top. Combine cinnamon and remaining sugar; sprinkle over rolls. Bake at 350 degrees for 30 minutes. Makes 8 to 10 servings.

Cinnamon-Pistachio Bread

Lucile Dahlberg
Glendale, CA

Sprinkle these loaves with a little extra cinnamon & sugar before baking them.

18-1/2 oz. pkg. yellow cake mix
3-oz. pkg. instant pistachio
   pudding mix
4 eggs
1/4 c. plus 1/2 t. oil

1/8 c. water
1 c. sour cream
1/4 c. chopped nuts
3 T. sugar
1-1/2 T. cinnamon

Combine all ingredients except sugar and cinnamon in a large bowl. Mix well; set aside. Divide sugar and cinnamon between 2 greased 8"x4-1/2" loaf pans; divide batter evenly between pans. Bake at 350 degrees for 45 minutes. Serve warm or cold. Makes 2 loaves.

Blissful Breakfasts

Creamy Ham Croissants

Lisa Johnson
Hallsville, TX

Brush rolls with a little beaten egg white before baking for a golden finish.

1-1/2 c. cooked ham, diced
8-oz. pkg. cream cheese,
   softened

12-oz. tube refrigerated
   crescent rolls

Mix ham and cream cheese in a bowl; set aside. Unroll and separate crescent rolls; place a spoonful of ham mixture on each. Roll up; place on an ungreased baking sheet. Bake for 15 to 18 minutes at 425 degrees. Makes 8 servings.

Yummy pancake and waffle syrup in your favorite fruit flavor!
Combine a small box of fruit-flavored gelatin, one cup water,
1/2 cup sugar and 2 tablespoons cornstarch in a saucepan.
Bring to a rolling boil, pour into a syrup pitcher
and let cool slightly before serving.

Crescent Sausage & Cheese Bake

Carol Brashear
Myerstown, PA

*This dish is a tradition at our family's Christmas brunch,
along with fresh fruit salad and hot tea and coffee.*

8-oz. tube refrigerated
    crescent rolls
1/2 lb. ground sausage,
    browned and drained
8-oz. pkg. shredded
    Cheddar cheese

5 eggs, beaten
3/4 c. milk
1/4 t. salt
1/8 t. pepper
1/4 t. dried oregano

Spread rolls in the bottom of a greased 13"x9" baking pan; press in bottom and halfway up sides of pan. Sprinkle sausage over crust; sprinkle with cheese. Combine remaining ingredients; blend well. Pour over cheese; bake at 425 degrees for 20 to 25 minutes. Serves 6 to 8.

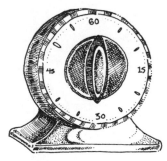

Company coming for brunch? Take it easy...the night before, mix up dry ingredients for muffins or waffles, chop veggies for omelets or whisk eggs for scrambling. The next day, you'll be a happy hostess.

No-Stress
Nibbling

Garlic Pretzels

Jo Anne Hayon
Sheboygan, WI

It's hard to stop eating these savory nuggets!

4 12-oz. pkgs. Bavarian-style
   pretzels, coarsely broken
12-oz. bottle butter-flavored
   popping oil

2 1-1/2 oz. pkgs. onion
   soup mix
2 t. garlic powder

Place pretzels in a large roasting pan; set aside. Combine remaining
ingredients; pour over pretzels to coat. Bake at 350 degrees for
20 minutes, stirring every 5 minutes. Lay on paper towels to cool.
Makes 6 cups.

Crispy Crunchy Snack Mix

Marcia Rae Buehrer
Stryker, OH

This makes a LOT of mix for tasty nibbling!
Great for big parties and for gifts too.

16-oz. pkg. corn chips
15-oz. bag pretzel twists
12-oz. pkg. oyster crackers
10-oz. pkg. baked wheat
   crackers
9-oz. pkg. thin wheat crackers
7-1/2 oz. pkg. savory baked
   crackers

5-oz. pkg. horn-shaped
   corn snacks
12-oz. can mixed nuts
12-oz. bottle butter-flavored
   popping oil
1-oz. pkg. ranch salad
   dressing mix

Combine all ingredients except oil and dressing mix in a very large
bowl; toss to mix and set aside. Warm oil; stir dressing mix into oil
with a fork until well dissolved. Drizzle over snack mixture; mix with
hands until well coated. Store in airtight containers; let stand for
several days to allow flavors to blend. Makes 3 gallons.

No-Stress Nibbling

Herbed Cheese Focaccia

Rita Morgan
Pueblo, CO

*A restaurant favorite, scrumptious for snacking
or to accompany a tossed salad.*

13.8-oz. tube refrigerated
   pizza dough
1 onion, finely chopped
2 cloves garlic, minced
2 T. olive oil

1 t. dried basil
1 t. dried oregano
1/2 t. dried rosemary
1 c. shredded mozzarella cheese

Unroll dough on a greased baking sheet. Press with fingers to form indentations; set aside. Sauté onion and garlic in oil in a skillet; remove from heat. Stir in herbs; spread mixture evenly over dough. Sprinkle with cheese. Bake at 400 degrees for 10 to 15 minutes, until golden. Serves 12 to 14.

Appetizer spreads are perfect for enjoying during card games
or a favorite movie at home with friends! Set out a variety of
creamy dips, crunchy snacks and sweet munchies
along with fizzy beverages.

Hot Feta-Artichoke Dip

Teresa Mulhern
University Heights, OH

This dip can be made ahead and refrigerated...just bake it a little longer.

14-oz. can artichokes, drained
   and chopped
2-oz. jar pimentos, drained
   and chopped
8-oz. pkg. crumbled feta cheese

1/2 c. grated Parmesan cheese
1 clove garlic, minced
1 c. mayonnaise
assorted snack crackers or
   tortilla chips

Mix all ingredients except crackers or chips. Spread in an ungreased 9" pie plate. Bake at 350 degrees for 20 to 25 minutes, until golden and bubbly. Serve with crackers or chips. Makes about 3 cups.

Savory Spinach Dip

DeNeane Deskins
Indian Harbor Beach, FL

Everyone's favorite dip...creamy and crunchy.

1-1/2-oz. pkg. vegetable
   soup mix
16-oz. container sour cream
1 c. mayonnaise
10-oz. pkg. frozen chopped
   spinach, thawed and drained

8-oz. can water chestnuts,
   drained and chopped
3 green onions, chopped
assorted snack crackers

Stir together soup mix, sour cream and mayonnaise until well blended; add remaining ingredients except crackers. Cover; chill for 2 hours before serving. Surround with crackers. Makes about 5 cups.

Stand up pretzel rods for dipping in a vase...takes up less table space.

No-Stress Nibbling

Robert's Corn Dip

Carole Snodgrass
Rolla, MO

*This dip is sooo delicious! The flavor is even better
if it's made 2 days ahead of time.*

3 11-oz. cans sweet corn &
   diced peppers, drained
7-oz. can chopped green chiles
6-oz. can chopped jalapeños,
   drained and liquid added
   to taste
1/2 c. green onion, chopped

1 c. mayonnaise
1 c. sour cream
1 t. pepper
1/2 t. garlic powder
16-oz. pkg. shredded sharp
   Cheddar cheese
corn chips

Mix all ingredients except corn chips together and refrigerate.
Serve with corn chips for scooping. Makes about 6 cups.

The secret to being a relaxed hostess...choose foods that can
be prepared in advance. At party time, simply pull from the
fridge and serve, or pop into a hot oven as needed.

Crabby Cheese Ball

Kathy Epperly
Wichita, KS

Add a dash of seafood seasoning for seaside flavor.

2 8-oz. pkgs. cream cheese,
   softened
.7-oz. pkg. Italian salad
   dressing mix

6-oz. can crabmeat, drained
1 c. chopped pecans
assorted snack crackers

Combine cream cheese, dressing mix and crabmeat. Blend well;
refrigerate for one to 2 hours. Form into a ball; roll in nuts. Arrange
on a serving plate, surrounded by crackers. Makes about 3-1/2 cups.

The next time a party guest asks, "How can I help?"
be ready with an answer! Whether it's picking up a bag
of ice, setting the table or even bringing a special dessert,
friends are usually happy to help.

No-Stress Nibbling

Seaside Shrimp Spread

Gladys Brehm
Quakertown, PA

An oversized shell makes a clever container for this creamy spread.

8-oz. pkg. cream cheese,
   softened
2 6-oz. cans tiny shrimp,
   drained

1 t. Worcestershire sauce
1 onion, finely chopped
carrot and celery sticks or
   snack crackers

Using an electric mixer on low speed, beat cream cheese until smooth. Set aside. Mash shrimp with a fork; combine with cream cheese, Worcestershire sauce and onion. Mix well; serve with vegetables or crackers. Makes about 2-1/2 cups.

Colorful, fresh veggies are always welcome at parties and easy to prepare in advance. Cut into sticks, flowerets or slices and tuck away in plastic zipping bags until needed.

Can't-Eat-One Bacon Swirls

Jan Swartzel
Canal Fulton, OH

Maybe you'd better double the recipe!

6 slices bacon, crisply cooked
  and crumbled
4-oz. can mushrooms,
  drained and chopped
1/4 c. mayonnaise
1/2 t. garlic powder

8-oz. tube refrigerated
  crescent rolls
2 3-oz. pkgs. cream cheese,
  softened
1 egg white, beaten
Garnish: poppy seed

Mix together bacon, mushrooms, mayonnaise and garlic powder;
set aside. Separate crescent rolls into 4 rectangles; press together
perforations. Spread rolls with cream cheese; top with bacon mixture.
Roll lengthwise; slice into one-inch pieces. Arrange on an ungreased
baking sheet. Brush with egg white; sprinkle with poppy seed.
Bake for 9 minutes at 375 degrees, until golden. Makes 3 dozen.

Check out what's new at the supermarket! You just may find
an old favorite in a new flavor to spice up a tried & true
recipe...cream soups, shredded cheese blends and salad
dressings, just to name a few.

No-Stress Nibbling

Reuben Rolls

Teresa Mulhern
University Heights, OH

*This appetizer is a favorite treat of my sister-in-law and myself
whenever we visit a quaint little local pub together.
We've spent the winter perfecting our own version of it.*

12-oz. can corned beef, sliced
  and shredded
8-oz. pkg. shredded Swiss
  cheese
2/3 c. sauerkraut, rinsed
  and drained

1/4 c. sweet onion, finely
  chopped
15 to 20 egg roll wrappers
oil for deep frying
Garnish: Thousand Island
  salad dressing

Combine corned beef, cheese, sauerkraut and onion in a bowl. Spoon
about 2 tablespoons of mixture into the center of each egg roll
wrapper. Fold sides of wrapper in and roll up egg-roll style, sealing
edges with water. Heat oil to 350 degrees in a deep saucepan.
Deep-fry rolls a few at a time until golden on all sides, 3 to 4 minutes.
Remove from oil with a slotted spoon; drain on paper towels. Serve
warm with salad dressing for dipping. Makes 15 to 20.

How do you know when oil is hot enough for deep frying?
Drop a bread cube into the hot oil. If it turns golden
in 60 seconds, the oil is ready.

Sweet Dill Pickles

Mary Baker
Bayonet Point, FL

These are so easy but taste like they've taken days to prepare.

2-qt. jar whole dill pickles,
    drained and liquid reserved

1 c. white vinegar
1-1/2 c. sugar

Slice pickles lengthwise or in chunks. Return slices to jar; add vinegar and sugar. Fill jar to top with reserved pickle liquid; screw on lid tightly. Turn jar upside-down until sugar dissolves. Let stand at room temperature for one week. Chill before serving. Makes 2 quarts.

Marinated Olives

Pat Geno
Everett, WA

My kids' favorite olive recipe...they ask for it at all holidays.
You'll probably want to double the recipe!

6-oz. can whole black olives,
    drained
1/4 c. olive oil
2 T. fresh oregano or basil,
    chopped

2 cloves garlic, minced
1 T. balsamic vinegar
1/2 t. red pepper flakes
1/4 t. salt

Combine all ingredients in a plastic zipping bag. Refrigerate at least 2 hours or up to one month. Makes about one cup.

Serving finger foods before dinner? Offer small bites like Marinated Olives that will pique guests' appetites but not fill them up.

No-Stress Nibbling

Mushroom Meatballs

Shirley Moench
Garfield, MN

A terrific appetizer...or stir in cream to make more gravy and serve over mashed potatoes or noodles as a main dish. Mmm!

2 10-3/4 oz. cans cream of
   mushroom soup
1-1/2 oz. pkg. onion soup mix

1 onion, chopped
2-lb. pkg. frozen meatballs,
   thawed

Stir first 3 ingredients well in a slow cooker; add meatballs. Cover and cook on high setting for 2 hours. Reduce heat to low setting and cook an additional 2 to 4 hours. Serves 6 to 8.

Use mini pretzel sticks instead of toothpicks to serve snacks
like meatballs or cheese cubes.

Mini Snacking Pizzas

*Kathleen White
Auburn, CA*

This is a great snack to keep on hand...both kids and adults love it. After spreading cheese mixture on bread, arrange slices on baking sheets and freeze uncovered, then store in plastic freezer bags. Bake frozen mini pizzas for 15 to 20 minutes.

16-oz. pkg. shredded sharp
   Cheddar cheese
16-oz. pkg. shredded
   mozzarella cheese
4-oz. can mushrooms, drained
   and chopped
2-oz. jar green olives with
   pimentos, drained and
   chopped

8-oz. can tomato sauce
1/2 c. oil
1 t. dried oregano
Worcestershire sauce to taste
garlic powder and cayenne
   pepper to taste
2 16-oz. loaves sliced party rye

Combine all ingredients except bread. Spread one tablespoon of mixture onto each slice of bread. Arrange on ungreased baking sheets; bake at 350 degrees for 10 to 15 minutes, until heated through and cheese melts. Makes about 4 dozen.

Nestle a bowl of creamy dip inside a larger bowl filled with crushed ice to keep it fresh and tasty.

No-Stress Nibbling

Baja Shrimp Quesadillas

Jo Ann

Cheesy, chewy, spicy shrimp bites!

2-1/2 lbs. shrimp, peeled
   and cleaned
3 c. shredded Cheddar cheese
1/2 c. mayonnaise
3/4 c. salsa

1/4 t. ground cumin
1/4 t. cayenne pepper
1/4 t. pepper
12 6-inch flour tortillas

Chop shrimp, discarding tails. Mix shrimp, cheese, mayonnaise, salsa, cumin and peppers; spread one to 2 tablespoons on one tortilla. Place another tortilla on top; put on a greased baking sheet. Repeat with remaining tortillas. Bake at 350 degrees for 15 minutes; remove and cut into triangles. Makes about 4 dozen.

Use muffin tins to make giant ice cubes for a punch bowl...they'll last much longer!

Black Bean Salsa

Kathy Epperly
Wichita, KS

Surround with a variety of tortilla chips...yellow, red and even blue.

15-oz. can black beans, drained
   and rinsed
8-oz. pkg. frozen corn, thawed
14-oz. can diced tomatoes with
   basil, garlic and oregano

10-oz. can tomatoes with chiles
8-oz. bottle Italian salad
   dressing
1 jalapeño, chopped
tortilla chips

Mix together all ingredients except chips; refrigerate for at least one to 2 hours. Serve with tortilla chips. Makes 5 to 6 cups.

Turn your favorite pork or beef barbecue recipe
into a delicious appetizer...simply arrange bite-size pieces
on skewers for easy snacking.

No-Stress Nibbling

Texas Caviar

Denise Bliss
Milton, NY

Spoon this dip into a colorful squash for serving.

16-oz. can black-eyed peas,
    drained and rinsed
15-oz. can shoepeg corn,
    drained
1/2 yellow pepper, chopped
1/2 orange pepper, chopped

1/2 c. sweet onion, chopped
1/4 c. oil
1/4 c. white vinegar
salt and pepper to taste
Optional: 1/4 c. sugar
tortilla chips

Combine vegetables in a serving bowl. Add remaining ingredients except chips; mix well. Cover and chill for at least one hour. Serve with tortilla chips. Makes 4-1/2 to 5 cups.

Try hollowed-out bread rounds, cabbage or even
pineapple halves for serving tasty dips.

Dilled Salmon Spread

Fawn McKenzie
Butte, MT

This spread is tasty on water crackers or thinly sliced bagels.

2 8-oz. pkgs. cream cheese,
   softened
3 T. lemon juice
3 T. milk

1-1/2 t. dill weed
2 6-oz. cans pink salmon,
   drained
1/4 c. green onion, thinly sliced

Blend cream cheese with lemon juice, milk and dill weed. Stir in salmon and green onion. Cover and chill for several hours to let flavors blend. Makes about 3-1/2 cups.

When people are true friends,
even shared water tastes sweet.

-Chinese proverb

No-Stress Nibbling

Cheddar-Blue Cheese Ball

Kay Swarthout
Vienna, MO

*My girlfriend shared this recipe with me more than
35 years ago...it's been a family favorite ever since!*

2 3-oz. pkgs. crumbled blue
cheese
2 5-oz. jars sharp pasteurized
processed cheese spread
4 3-oz. pkgs. cream cheese,
softened

1 t. Worcestershire sauce
1/4 c. dried parsley
Garnish: chopped nuts
snack crackers, sliced fruit

Combine cheeses, Worcestershire sauce and parsley; mix well. Form
into a ball and roll in chopped nuts. Wrap in plastic wrap; refrigerate
for 2 days to allow flavors to blend. At serving time, let stand at room
temperature to soften. Serve with a variety of crackers or fruit for
dipping. Makes 3-1/2 to 4 cups.

For stand-up parties, make it easy on guests by serving foods
that can be eaten in one or 2 bites.

Creamy Artichoke Pizzas

Kelly Fitzmorris
Lawrence, KS

For smaller appetizers, substitute 6 mini pizza crusts.

2 12-inch Italian pizza crusts
14-oz. can artichoke hearts,
   drained and chopped
8-oz. pkg. cream cheese,
   softened

1 c. grated Parmesan cheese
1/2 c. mayonnaise
3/4 t. dill weed
1 clove garlic, minced

Place pizza crusts on 2 ungreased baking sheets; set aside. Mix together remaining ingredients; spread onto crusts. Bake for 10 to 12 minutes at 450 degrees. Cut into wedges. Makes 12 servings.

Fresh herbs give a wonderful flavor boost to foods!
For one teaspoon of a dried herb like dill or rosemary,
simply substitute one tablespoon of the fresh herb.

No-Stress Nibbling

Italian Egg Rolls

Carolyn Scilabro
Hampton, VA

Slice in half diagonally for easy-to-eat appetizer portions.

1/2 c. onion, chopped
1/2 c. green pepper, chopped
2 t. oil
1 lb. ground sweet or
   hot Italian sausage
2 10-oz. pkgs. frozen spinach,
   thawed and drained

1/2 c. grated Parmesan cheese
3 c. shredded mozzarella cheese
1/2 t. garlic powder
14-oz. pkg. egg roll wrappers
olive oil for deep frying
Garnish: pizza sauce

In a skillet, sauté onion and pepper in oil; remove to a medium bowl
and set aside. Brown sausage in skillet; drain and combine with onion
mixture. Add spinach, cheeses and garlic powder; mix well. Top each
egg roll wrapper with about 3 tablespoons of mixture; roll up
following directions on egg roll package. Heat 3 to 4 inches oil in a
deep fryer; add a few egg rolls at a time, frying until golden. Drain on
paper towels. Serve warm with pizza sauce for dipping. Makes 8.

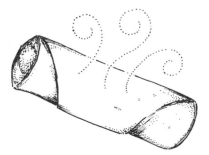

Dress up the serving table with pictures and paper cut-outs
for the occasion...try travel brochures and maps for a
going-away party or playing cards for a card party. Lay
heavy clear plastic over all and voilá! Aren't you clever!

Mini Ham & Swiss Cups

Shari Miller
Hobart, IN

This appetizer is perfect for a shower, brunch or anytime!
I'm always asked for the recipe.

2-1/2 oz. pkg. deli ham,
   finely chopped
1 onion, finely chopped
1/2 c. shredded Swiss cheese
1 egg, beaten

1/2 t. Dijon mustard
1/8 t. pepper
8-oz. tube refrigerated
   crescent rolls

Combine ham and onion; add cheese, egg, mustard and pepper.
Mix well and set aside. Unroll crescent rolls; press dough into a
single large rectangle. Cut rectangle into 24 squares. Press dough
into 24 lightly greased mini muffin cups. Fill muffin cups with ham
mixture. Bake at 350 degrees for 13 to 15 minutes, or until golden.
Makes 2 dozen.

The simplest spreads can be the most welcome! Set out a
honey-baked ham along with condiments, small bread rolls
and some crunchy veggies. Guests will love helping
themselves to mini sandwiches.

No-Stress Nibbling

Mini BLT's

Tami Bowman
Gooseberry Patch

Try using fresh basil leaves in place of lettuce for a savory treat.

17.3-oz. tube refrigerated golden wheat biscuits 1/2 c. mayonnaise	4 lettuce leaves 8 tomato slices 1 lb. bacon, crisply cooked

Separate dough into 8 biscuits; flatten each into a 5-1/2 inch circle. Arrange on a lightly greased baking sheet. Bake at 350 degrees for 16 to 18 minutes, or until golden. Let biscuits cool; split open. Spread one tablespoon mayonnaise on split side of each biscuit. Top each of 4 biscuits with a lettuce leaf, 2 tomato slices and 4 to 5 slices of bacon. Top with remaining biscuits, mayonnaise side down. For appetizers, slice each sandwich into quarters and spear with cocktail picks. Makes 16.

Cut cheese into fun shapes with tiny cookie cutters...a clever touch for an appetizer platter.

Nacho Chicken Dip

Trudy Williams
Middlesex, NC

We love this delicious dip at parties...it's even good as a meal, paired with a side salad.

16-oz. can refried beans
12-oz. can chicken, drained
16-oz. jar chunky salsa

8-oz. pkg. shredded Mexican-
    blend cheese
tortilla chips

Layer beans, chicken, salsa and cheese in a lightly greased 9" round baking pan. Bake at 350 degrees for 30 minutes, or until cheese is bubbly. Serve hot with tortilla chips. Makes about 6-1/2 cups.

Make a delicious buffet even more inviting...arrange inverted cake pans or bowls on the table to create different levels. Cover all with a tablecloth and set food platters on top.

No-Stress Nibbling

Summery Taco Dip

Rachael Gingras
Townsend, MA

*A clear glass dish shows off the colored layers and
makes the prettiest presentation.*

16-oz. container sour cream
8-oz. pkg. cream cheese,
   softened
16-oz. jar chunky salsa

1 red onion, chopped
2 tomatoes, chopped
2 green peppers, chopped
tortilla chips

Blend together sour cream and cream cheese; spread in the bottom of
a 13"x9" glass baking pan. Spread with salsa; set aside. Mix together
onion, tomatoes and peppers; spread over top. Surround with tortilla
chips. Makes about 10 cups.

Frosty glasses make cold drinks extra tasty...nestle mugs or
stemmed glasses in ice until serving time.

Golden Parmesan Wedges

Jennifer Bishoff
Swanton, MD

A nice change from ordinary bread sticks!

6-1/2 oz. pkg. pizza crust mix
3 T. butter, melted
1/4 to 1/2 c. grated Parmesan
   cheese
garlic powder to taste

Italian seasoning to taste
1 c. shredded mozzarella cheese
Garnish: ranch salad dressing,
   marinara sauce

Prepare pizza dough as directed on package; roll out on an ungreased 12" pizza pan. Brush dough with melted butter. Sprinkle with Parmesan cheese, garlic powder and Italian seasoning; top with mozzarella cheese. Bake as package directs; cut into wedges. Serve with ranch dressing and marinara sauce for dipping. Serves 4 to 6.

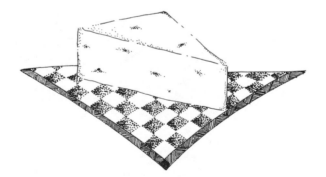

An instant appetizer...set out a warm loaf of Italian bread
and a little dish of olive oil sprinkled with
Italian seasoning for dipping.

No-Stress Nibbling

Pull-Apart Pizza Bread

Sallyann Cortese
Sewickley, PA

Some of my English students gave me this easy recipe and a tasty sample...they'd just baked it in their Home Ec class.

12-oz. tube refrigerated flaky
   biscuits, quartered
1 T. olive oil
12 slices pepperoni, quartered
1/4 c. shredded mozzarella
   cheese

1 onion, chopped
1 t. Italian seasoning
1/4 t. garlic salt
1/4 c. grated Parmesan cheese

Brush biscuits with oil; set aside. Combine remaining ingredients in a bowl; add biscuits. Toss well; arrange in a Bundt® pan lined with well-greased aluminum foil. Bake at 400 degrees for 15 minutes. Pull bread apart to serve. Makes about 2 dozen pieces.

Italian Sausage Bread

Sally Langford
Lorain, OH

Try adding onions or any other pizza toppings you enjoy.

1 loaf frozen French bread
   dough, thawed
1 lb. ground Italian sausage,
   browned and drained

Optional: 4-oz. can sliced
   mushrooms, drained
Optional: 12 slices pepperoni
3 c. shredded mozzarella cheese

Roll dough out on a greased baking sheet; sprinkle with sausage, mushrooms and pepperoni, if using, and cheese. Roll up; pinch seams together. Bake at 400 degrees for 20 to 25 minutes, or until golden; cool for at least 15 minutes. Makes one dozen slices.

A 250-degree oven keeps hot appetizers toasty.

Mini Wonton Salsa Baskets

Jo Ann

These crisp shells are a good container for creamy shrimp spread too.

24 wonton wrappers
15-1/4 oz. can corn, drained
16-oz. can black beans, drained
   and rinsed

16-oz. can kidney beans,
   drained and rinsed
8-oz. jar salsa
1 c. shredded Cheddar cheese

Spray 24 mini muffin cups with non-stick vegetable spray; press a
wonton wrapper into each cup. Bake at 350 degrees for 10 minutes,
until crisp. Mix together corn, beans and salsa; spoon into cups. Top
with cheese. Makes 2 dozen.

For a fast and fun party punch, combine a pint of sherbet
with a 2-liter bottle of chilled soda. Match up
flavors...strawberry sherbet with strawberry soda,
lime sherbet with lemon-lime soda. Yummy!

No-Stress Nibbling

Black & White Bean Dip

Denise Bliss
Milton, NY

A refreshing appetizer, especially good on hot summer days.

16-oz. can black beans, drained
   and rinsed
16-oz. can white beans, drained
   and rinsed
14-1/2 oz. can stewed tomatoes
1/4 c. green onion, chopped

1/4 c. fresh cilantro, chopped
1 T. lime juice
salt, pepper and ground cumin
   to taste
tortilla chips

Combine all ingredients except tortilla chips; mix well. Chill for at least one hour. Serve with tortilla chips. Makes about 5-1/2 cups.

Planning an appetizers-only event? You'll want to serve at least 5 different dishes...allow 2 to 3 servings of each per person.

Ham & Cheese Pinwheels

Kathleen Popp
Oak Harbor, WA

Easily frozen and reheated...good to keep on hand for impromptu get-togethers.

16-oz. pkg. hot roll mix
1/4 c. butter, softened
1-oz. pkg. ranch salad
   dressing mix

1 c. shredded Cheddar cheese
1/2 lb. thinly sliced deli ham

Prepare hot roll mix according to package directions; knead dough 10 times on a well-floured surface. Roll into an 18-inch by 12-inch rectangle; set aside. Mix butter and dressing mix; spread on dough. Sprinkle with cheese; arrange ham slices over cheese. Starting at long edge of dough, roll up jelly-roll style. Pinch raw edges together; place seam-side down on a greased baking sheet. Pinch ends together. Snip top of dough at 2-inch intervals. Let rise until double in bulk, 45 minutes to one hour. Bake at 325 degrees for 40 to 50 minutes, until golden. Slice to serve. Makes 16 servings.

For an elegant yet quick last-minute appetizer, toss a drained jar of Italian antipasto mix with bite-size cubes of mozzarella or provolone cheese. Serve with cocktail picks.

No-Stress Nibbling

Golden Fortune Egg Rolls

Audrey Lett
Newark, DE

*Your friends will love these hearty egg rolls...try 'em
with hot chili sauce.*

1 lb. ground sausage, browned
   and drained
2 16-oz. pkgs. coleslaw mix
3 T. fresh ginger, peeled and
   minced
3 T. garlic, finely chopped

1 T. pepper
1 t. salt
18 to 20 egg roll wrappers
oil for deep frying
Garnish: spicy mustard,
   sweet-and-sour sauce

Combine browned sausage, coleslaw mix, ginger, garlic, pepper and
salt in a large bowl; mix well. Place in a colander and let drain for
15 minutes. Assemble egg rolls according to package directions, using
1/3 cup sausage mixture for each; set aside. Heat 3 inches oil to
375 degrees in a wok, Dutch oven or deep fryer. Fry egg rolls 3 to
4 at a time until golden, about 3 minutes. Drain on paper towels.
Serve with sauces for dipping. Makes 18 to 20.

Sparkling fruit juice served in stemmed glasses makes a
festive beverage that even youngsters can enjoy.

Crab Rangoon

Betty Gretch
Owendale, MI

These always disappear quickly at family gatherings...luckily they are very easy to make.

8-oz. pkg. cream cheese,
   softened
6-oz. can crabmeat, drained

1/8 t. garlic salt
14-oz. pkg. wonton wrappers
oil for deep frying

Combine cream cheese, crabmeat and garlic salt in a bowl. Stir until blended. Separate wrappers and lightly moisten around edges with water. Place 1/2 teaspoon of cheese mixture in center of each wrapper; bring corners of wrapper together and seal well. Deep-fry until golden. Makes 1-1/2 dozen.

Arrange baby veggies in a cornucopia basket for dipping! Cherry tomatoes, snow peas, baby corn and mini mushrooms are all pleasing to the eye as well as the palate.

Soups & Salads in a Snap

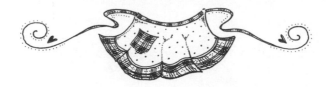

Creamy Ranch Macaroni Salad

Dawn Wetherington
Kankakee, IL

Spoon into ripe tomato cups for a cool summer lunch.

16-oz. pkg. medium shell pasta,
  uncooked
3/4 c. onion, chopped
1/2 c. celery, chopped
1 c. fresh Italian parsley,
  chopped

1 c. sour cream
1-oz. pkg. ranch salad dressing
  mix, divided
1 c. mayonnaise
1/2 c. shredded Cheddar cheese

Cook shells according to package directions; drain and rinse with cold water. Set aside. Combine onion, celery and parsley in a large bowl; add shells and toss together. Add sour cream and half the salad dressing mix; stir well. Add mayonnaise and remaining dressing mix; stir again. Toss with Cheddar cheese. Serves 8 to 10.

Keep color and texture contrasts in mind as you plan dinner. For example, crispy, golden fried chicken teamed with creamy white macaroni salad and juicy red tomato slices...everything will taste twice as good!

Rainbow Pasta Salad

Melissa Phillips
Provo, UT

Perfect for a potluck or a family reunion!

16-oz. pkg. rainbow rotini,
    uncooked
6-oz. can black olives, drained
    and sliced
1 green pepper, chopped
1 red pepper, chopped
1 cucumber, chopped
1 c. pepperoni, sliced and
    quartered
16-oz. bottle Italian salad
    dressing, divided

Cook rotini according to package directions; drain and rinse with cold water. Mix together rotini and all ingredients except dressing in a large bowl. Pour half the salad dressing over the top; toss to coat. Chill. Stir in remaining dressing at serving time. Serves 8 to 10.

For chilled salads, cook pasta for the shortest time given
on the package, then rinse with cold water.
Drain well...no mushy macaroni!

Chicken Corn Chowder

Katie French
Portland, OR

My husband's favorite soup…it's delicious with cornbread.

1-1/2 c. milk
10-1/2 oz. can chicken broth
10-3/4 oz. can cream of
   chicken soup
10-3/4 oz. can cream of
   potato soup
1 to 2 10-oz. cans chicken,
   drained

1/3 c. green onion, chopped
11-oz. can sweet corn & diced
   peppers
4-oz. can chopped green chiles,
   drained
8-oz. pkg. shredded Cheddar
   cheese

Mix together all ingredients except cheese in a 6-quart saucepan. Heat over low heat, stirring frequently, for about 15 minutes, until heated through. Add cheese; stir until melted. Serves 6 to 8.

Save extra broth by freezing in an ice cube tray or muffin tin. Add the broth cubes when cooking rice or veggies…a real flavor boost.

Green Bean Salad

Karol Floyd
Sharpsville, IN

A colorful make-ahead salad...most welcome on buffet tables.

2 14-1/2 oz. cans French-style
    green beans, drained
15-oz. can peas, drained
1 green pepper, chopped
1 c. celery, chopped

1 red onion, chopped
2-oz. jar pimentos, drained
1-1/2 c. sugar
1 c. cider vinegar
1/2 c. oil

Mix vegetables in a salad bowl; set aside. Combine sugar, vinegar and oil in a jar; cover and shake well. Pour over salad; toss to mix. Refrigerate 24 hours; drain or use a slotted spoon to serve. Makes 6 to 8 servings.

Onions are delicious in salads. For a milder flavor, cover sliced onion with cold water and a splash of vinegar for half an hour before using.

Mexican 3-Bean Soup

Kathy Mathews
Byers, TX

*This soup freezes wonderfully. Often I make a double batch
and freeze individual portions for quick lunches.*

1 lb. ground beef
1 onion, diced
2 15-1/2 oz. cans kidney beans
2 16-oz. cans pinto beans
2 15-1/2 oz. cans navy beans
15-oz. can corn
14-1/2 oz. can stewed tomatoes

14-1/2 oz. can tomatoes
  with chiles
1-1/4 oz. pkg. taco
  seasoning mix
1-oz. pkg. ranch salad
  dressing mix

Brown meat and onion over medium heat in a Dutch oven; drain.
Add remaining ingredients; simmer over low heat for one hour.
Serves 8 to 10.

Make veggie or bean soups thick & creamy...simply purée
a cup or so of the soup in a blender, then stir it
back into the soup pot.

Shoepeg Corn Salad

Mida Pilcher
Wichita Falls, TX

Don't discard the celery leaves! Chop finely and add to soups or salads for extra flavor.

2 11-oz. cans shoepeg corn,
   drained
2 stalks celery, diced
1/4 c. onion, chopped
1 green or red pepper, diced

8-oz. container sour cream
1/2 c. Caesar salad dressing
salt and pepper to taste
garnish: paprika

Mix the first 6 ingredients together. Add salt and pepper to taste; garnish with paprika. Chill. Serves 4 to 6.

Stash bags of fresh salad greens in the fridge along with chopped veggies and even crispy bacon left from breakfast. Toss with dressing for a salad ready in a flash!

Caesar Shrimp Salad

Dorothy Benson
Baton Rouge, LA

Friends & family will "ooh" & "aah" over this delicious salad.

2 lbs. medium shrimp,
   peeled and cleaned
3 cloves garlic, finely chopped
1/4 c. olive oil
3 hearts romaine lettuce,
   torn into bite-size pieces
5-oz. pkg. spring greens mix

5-oz. pkg. baby spinach
16-oz. pkg. shredded
   mozzarella cheese
16-oz. bottle Caesar
   salad dressing
5-oz. pkg. Caesar salad croutons
Optional: cherry tomatoes

In a skillet over medium heat, sauté shrimp and garlic in oil just until cooked through, 5 to 10 minutes. Remove shrimp; cover and chill. Toss together romaine, spring greens and spinach in a medium bowl. Layer greens mixture, shrimp, cheese and dressing in a large salad bowl; repeat layering until bowl is full. Sprinkle croutons on top; garnish with cherry tomatoes, if desired. Serves 10 to 12.

A crisp, green salad is a refreshing start to dinner. Avoid soggy salads...simply pour salad dressing in the bottom of a salad bowl, then add greens on top. Toss just before serving...fresh and crisp!

Creamy Tomato Soup

Flo Burtnett
Gage, OK

The perfect partner for a grilled cheese sandwich.

1 onion, chopped
2 T. margarine
2 14-1/2 oz. cans diced
    tomatoes
2 10-3/4 oz. cans tomato soup
1-1/2 c. milk

1 t. sugar
1/2 t. dried basil
1/2 t. paprika
1/8 t. garlic powder
8-oz. pkg. cream cheese, cubed

In a large saucepan, sauté onion in margarine over medium heat until tender. Stir in remaining ingredients except cream cheese; bring to a boil. Reduce heat; cover and simmer for 10 minutes. Stir in cream cheese and heat until melted; serve immediately. Serves 8.

Keep cans of evaporated milk in the cupboard
to use in soups and gravies that call for regular
milk...extra creamy and needs no refrigeration.

Olive Antipasto Salad

Doreen Freiman
Lake Hiawatha, NJ

This salad will last for 10 days, refrigerated in a covered container.
The flavor gets even better the longer it marinates.

1/2 lb. large green Spanish
    olives, pitted
4 stalks celery, diced
1/4 lb. salami, diced
1/4 lb. provolone cheese, diced

2 12-oz. jars gardenia mix,
    drained
2 6-oz. jars artichoke hearts
    in marinade
1/2 c. white vinegar

Combine all ingredients in a large container, including marinade from
artichokes; mix well. Cover tightly and refrigerate at least 24 hours,
stirring occasionally. Makes 18 to 20 servings.

Kitchen scissors are a handy helper. Grab 'em to make
quick work of cutting up fresh herbs, dried fruits and
what-have-you...cut right into the bowl!

Italian Bean Soup

Julia Koons
Centerville, IN

*My boys love this soup! I always serve it with
plenty of French bread and creamy butter.*

1 lb. ground sausage
1 onion, chopped
1 clove garlic, minced
28-oz. can diced tomatoes
15-oz. can red kidney beans,
   drained and rinsed
14-1/2 oz. can beef broth

15-oz. can black beans, drained
   and rinsed
15-oz. can navy beans, drained
   and rinsed
2 T. grated Parmesan cheese
1 t. dried basil

Brown together sausage, onion and garlic in a stockpot over medium heat; drain. Add remaining ingredients; cook until soup comes to a boil. Serves 4 to 6.

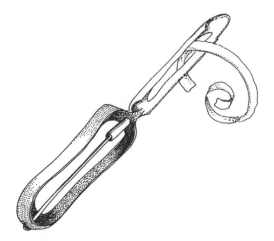

Use a vegetable peeler to make cheese curls
for a tasty garnish on soups and salads.

Smoky Sausage Soup

Lynda McCormick
Burkburnett, TX

A meal in itself, made from ingredients that are
easy to keep on hand. Perfect for winter days!

14-1/2 oz. can Italian stewed
   tomatoes
14-1/2 oz. can beef broth
1-1/2 c. water
10-oz. pkg. frozen mixed
   vegetables

2 c. frozen diced potatoes
1/2 lb. smoked sausage, sliced
1/2 t. pepper
Garnish: grated Parmesan
   cheese

Stir together stewed tomatoes, broth and water in a stockpot; bring to
a boil. Stir in vegetables, potatoes, sausage and pepper. Return to a boil;
reduce heat and cover. Simmer for 5 to 10 minutes. Serve sprinkled
with Parmesan cheese. Serves 4.

Add big, fluffy dumplings to your favorite stew...easy!
When the stew is nearly finished cooking, top with
refrigerated biscuits and continue simmering
10 to 15 minutes, until done.

Italian Bean & Tomato Salad

Kimberly Boyce
Murrieta, CA

Blanching gives the fresh green beans bright color. Simply drop the beans into boiling water just until tender, then immerse in ice water.

2 c. green beans, cut into one-
    inch pieces and blanched
2 15-oz. cans cannellini beans,
    drained and rinsed

2 c. roma tomatoes, chopped
1/2 c. Italian salad dressing
2 T. grated Parmesan cheese
2 T. fresh basil, chopped

Combine beans, tomatoes and dressing in a large bowl; toss to mix. Refrigerate for at least one hour. Sprinkle with cheese and basil just before serving. Makes about 6 servings.

Fill a big box with festive party napkins, candles
and table decorations...when surprise guests pop in,
you'll be all set to turn an ordinary dinner
into a special occasion.

Better-Than-Deli Linguine Salad

Tammy Rowe
Bellevue, OH

A delicious accompaniment to deli-style sandwiches of cold cuts on crusty rolls.

8-oz. pkg. linguine, uncooked
8-oz. bottle Italian salad
   dressing
3.8-oz. can sliced black olives,
   drained

1 tomato, chopped
1 green pepper, chopped
1 cucumber, chopped
3 green onions, chopped
3 T. salad seasoning

Cook linguine according to package directions; drain and rinse with cold water. Combine linguine with remaining ingredients in a large bowl. Chill overnight. Serves 6 to 8.

Look for all kinds of fresh, ready-to-use veggies on your supermarket's salad bar. Buy just what you need...dinner preparation is a snap!

Quick Minestrone

Diane Darr
Eureka, MO

This soup is loaded with "good for you" ingredients! I like to use combination bags of frozen veggies like carrots, celery, zucchini and onion...takes all the work out of making hearty soup!

2 14-1/2 oz. cans chicken broth
2 c. water
28-oz. can diced tomatoes
15-1/2 oz. can kidney beans,
    drained and rinsed

3 c. frozen vegetable blend
1 c. medium shell pasta,
    uncooked
Garnish: grated Parmesan
    cheese

Combine broth, water and vegetables in a large saucepan. Bring to a boil; add pasta. Reduce heat, cover and simmer for 20 to 25 minutes. Sprinkle servings generously with Parmesan cheese. Serves 10 to 12.

Does the soup taste just a little bland?
Add extra zing with a spoonful of balsamic vinegar
or perk it up with a bouillon cube or 2.

Chunky Pea Salad

Jaimie Schmutz
Dickson, TN

Slice Cheddar cheese into tiny cubes for a different look.

1 lb. bacon, crisply cooked
   and crumbled
6 eggs, hard-boiled,
   peeled and chopped
2 32-oz. pkgs. frozen peas,
   thawed and well drained

8-oz. pkg. shredded
   Cheddar cheese
1/2 c. red onion, chopped
1/2 to 1 c. mayonnaise

Combine all ingredients except mayonnaise in a large bowl. Add enough mayonnaise to moisten. Refrigerate for at least 4 hours; serve chilled. Makes 10 to 15 servings.

Zesty Cannellini Bean Salad

Carol Lytle
Columbus, OH

Cannellini beans are also sold as white kidney beans.
If you can't find them, simply substitute Great Northern beans.

2 15-oz. cans cannellini beans,
   drained and rinsed
1 green pepper, diced
1 red onion, sliced
1/4 c. fresh parsley, chopped

1/3 c. wine vinegar
3/4 c. olive oil
1 clove garlic, pressed
1 T. fresh chives, chopped
1/2 t. pepper

Combine beans, green pepper, onion and parsley in a large bowl. Blend together remaining ingredients and pour over bean mixture. Mix thoroughly, cover and chill well. Serves 4 to 6.

Dice bacon before cooking if it will be crumbled
for your recipe...it'll fry up quicker.

Soups & Salads in a snap

Au Gratin Potato Soup

Leona Toland
Baltimore, MD

*For a smooth, creamy soup simply purée in a blender,
then reheat if necessary before serving. Top with a dollop of
sour cream and a sprinkling of chopped fresh chives.*

9-oz. pkg. au gratin potato mix
10-1/2 oz. can chicken broth
3 c. water
2/3 c. carrots, diced

2/3 c. celery, diced
1 onion, diced
1/2 c. whipping cream
salt and pepper to taste

Mix the first 6 ingredients together in a saucepan; bring to a boil.
Reduce heat to a simmer; cover. Simmer for 30 minutes, or until
potatoes are tender; remove from heat. Stir in cream; sprinkle with
salt and pepper. Serves 6 to 8.

Soups taste even better
the next day...why not
make a double batch?
Let it cool thoroughly,
then cover and
refrigerate for up to
3 days. Supper tonight,
an easy lunch later on.

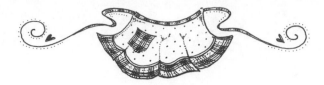

Easy Taco Soup

Jen Burnham
Delaware, OH

Perfect with a basket of corn or tortilla chips instead of crackers.

1 lb. ground beef
1 onion, chopped
1-1/2 c. water
15-1/4 oz. can corn
3 15-1/2 oz. cans Mexican
   chili beans
15-oz. can tomato sauce
14-1/2 oz. can diced tomatoes

4-1/2 oz. can chopped
   green chiles
1-1/4 oz. pkg. taco
   seasoning mix
Garnish: shredded lettuce,
   chopped tomato, shredded
   Cheddar cheese, sour cream

Place ground beef and onion in a Dutch oven over medium heat. Cook until beef is browned and onion is tender, stirring to break up meat. Drain. Stir in remaining ingredients except garnish; bring to a boil. Reduce heat and simmer, uncovered, for 15 minutes, stirring occasionally. Spoon soup into bowls; top with desired toppings. Serves 6 to 8.

Freeze extra Taco Soup or Chili in small containers...pop in the microwave for taco salads, chili dogs or nachos at a moment's notice.

Confetti Corn Salad

Karen Woodard
Meridianville, AL

Fresh garden veggies make this salad
a natural for summer cookouts.

3 12-oz. cans shoepeg corn, drained
3 tomatoes, seeded and chopped
2 green peppers, chopped
2 cucumbers, peeled, seeded and chopped
1 red onion, diced

1 c. sour cream
1/2 c. mayonnaise
1/4 c. white vinegar
2 t. salt
1 t. pepper
1 t. celery seed
1 t. dry mustard

Toss together vegetables in a large bowl; set aside. Combine remaining ingredients in a separate bowl; pour over vegetables, stirring to coat. Cover and refrigerate overnight; stir just before serving. Makes 18 to 20 servings.

Make a ho-hum salad special with the right garnish.
Add a sprinkle of fresh chives or basil for flavor
and sunflower kernels or homemade croutons
for extra texture.

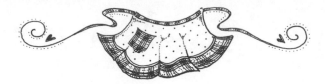

Fiesta Garden Salad

Angela Murphy
Tempe, AZ

Spoon individual portions into hollowed-out red peppers.

7 c. romaine lettuce leaves, torn
15-1/2 oz. can black beans,
   drained and rinsed
8-oz. pkg. shredded Monterey
   Jack cheese

15-oz. can corn, drained
1 green pepper, chopped
2 green onions, thinly sliced
3/4 c. creamy lime-cilantro
   salad dressing

In a large serving bowl, combine all ingredients except dressing.
Just before serving, toss with dressing. Makes 4 to 6 servings.

Lettuce won't brown if you tear it by hand
instead of cutting with a knife.

Nacho Potato Soup

Nancy Swindle
Winnemucca, NV

Stir in an extra spoonful of diced chiles for a spicier soup.

5-1/4 oz. pkg. au gratin
   potato mix
11-oz. can corn, drained
10-oz. can tomatoes with chiles

2 c. water
2 c. milk
2 c. American cheese, cubed

In a 3-quart saucepan, combine contents of potato mix, including cheese sauce, with corn, tomatoes and water. Mix well; bring to a boil. Reduce heat, cover and simmer for 15 to 18 minutes, until potatoes are tender. Add milk and cheese; cook and stir until cheese is melted. Serves 6 to 8.

Drain veggies very well in a colander before combining with salad dressing...the flavorful dressing won't be diluted.

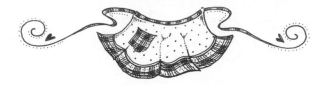

Quick & Easy Chicken Noodle Soup

Debbie Dunham
Lumberton, TX

Homemade chicken soup, ready in just a few minutes!

10 c. water
10 cubes chicken bouillon
2 10-1/2 oz. cans chicken,
   drained
10-3/4 oz. can cream of
   chicken soup

10-3/4 oz. can cream of
   celery soup
1-1/2 oz. pkg. onion soup mix
8-oz. pkg. wide egg noodles,
   uncooked

Bring water to a boil in a stockpot; add bouillon cubes and boil until dissolved. Add chicken, soups and soup mix; return to a boil. Stir in noodles; bring back to a boil. Reduce heat and simmer until noodles are tender, 8 to 12 minutes. Makes 8 to 10 servings.

Wrap up the ingredients for Quick & Easy Chicken Noodle Soup in a basket with a big napkin and deliver to someone who's under the weather...tie on the recipe with a raffia bow. How thoughtful!

Caesar Coleslaw

Lori Rosenberg
University Heights, OH

*Make packaged coleslaw mix crispier...soak it in ice water
for an hour, then drain well and pat dry.*

16-oz. pkg. coleslaw mix
1 c. red onion, thinly sliced
2/3 c. grated Parmesan cheese

1 c. creamy Caesar salad
   dressing
1 c. Caesar salad croutons

Combine coleslaw, onion and cheese in a large salad bowl; mix well.
Add salad dressing as desired; toss to coat. Add croutons and mix
thoroughly. Refrigerate for 4 to 6 hours. Makes about 14 servings.

Lacy cheese crisps are a tasty garnish for green salads.
Sprinkle freshly grated Parmesan cheese by the
tablespoon, 4 inches apart, onto a baking sheet lined with
parchment paper. Bake for 5 to 7 minutes at 400 degrees
until melted and golden, then cool.

Layered Spinach Salad

Debra Alf
Robbinsdale, MN

The tortellini makes this a heartier salad.

8-oz. pkg. cheese tortellini,
   uncooked
2 c. red cabbage, shredded
6 c. spinach leaves, torn
1 c. cherry tomatoes, halved

1/2 c. green onion, sliced
8-oz. bottle ranch salad dressing
8 slices bacon, crisply cooked
   and crumbled

Cook tortellini according to package directions; drain and rinse with
cold water. In a clear glass 13"x9" baking pan, layer cabbage, spinach,
tortellini, tomatoes and green onion. Pour dressing evenly over top;
sprinkle with bacon. Makes 8 servings.

It's easy to make fresh croutons for salads and soups!
Toss bread cubes with olive oil and dried herbs or garlic
powder as you like. Toast on a baking sheet at
400 degrees for 5 to 10 minutes, until golden.

Soups & Salads in a snap

World's Easiest Black Bean Soup

Joyce Jordan
Hurricane, WV

Serve with garlic toast or cornbread, or spoon over rice.

10-3/4 oz. can French
   onion soup
16-oz. can black beans,
   drained and rinsed

14-1/2 oz. can tomatoes
   with chiles
1-1/4 c. water
salt and pepper to taste

Combine all ingredients in a saucepan; heat to boiling. Reduce heat; simmer for 15 minutes. Makes 6 to 8 servings.

Lit candles are a quick way to add warmth and charm to a table setting. Make the most of their soft glow by setting candles on mirrors.

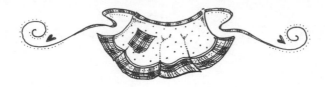

Tomato-Tortellini Soup

Diane Bailey
Red Lion, PA

Warm and comforting on a cold day.

1 T. margarine
3 cloves garlic, minced
3 10-1/2 oz. cans chicken broth
8-oz. pkg. cheese tortellini
1/4 c. grated Parmesan cheese
salt and pepper to taste

2/3 c. frozen chopped spinach,
   thawed and drained
14-1/2 oz. can Italian stewed
   tomatoes
1/2 c. tomato sauce

Melt margarine in a saucepan over medium heat; add garlic. Sauté for 2 minutes; stir in broth and tortellini. Bring to a boil; reduce heat. Mix in Parmesan cheese, salt and pepper; simmer until tortellini is tender. Stir in spinach, tomatoes and tomato sauce; simmer for 5 minutes. Serves 8 to 10.

There is only one difference between a long life and a good dinner: that in the dinner, the sweets don't last.

-Robert Louis Stevenson

Soups & Salads in a snap

Hearty Cobb Salad

Peggy Donnally
Toledo, OH

*Arrange the various ingredients in rows
or circles...almost too pretty to eat!*

16-oz. pkg. mixed salad greens
   or romaine lettuce
2 c. cooked chicken breast, diced
4 eggs, hard-boiled, peeled and
   cut into wedges
6 slices bacon, crisply cooked
   and crumbled

2 avocados, diced
3/4 c. crumbled blue cheese
4 to 6 green onions, sliced
15-oz. can baby corn, drained
8-oz. bottle buttermilk salad
   dressing

Arrange greens in a large salad bowl. Top with ingredients in order
listed. Toss lightly just before serving. Makes 6 to 8 servings.

Here's a fun way to serve fruit salads...line mini berry
baskets with aluminum foil, then with lettuce leaves
before spooning in salad.

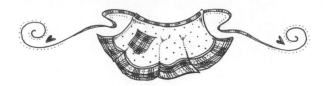

Spicy Vegetable Soup

Patricia Dammrich
St. Louis, MO

It's so easy to stir up a big pot of this delicious soup.

1 lb. ground beef
1 c. onion, chopped
1 c. celery, chopped
2 cloves garlic, minced
30-oz. jar chunky garden style
    spaghetti sauce
10-oz. can tomatoes with chiles
10-oz. pkg. frozen mixed
    vegetables

2 potatoes, peeled and cubed
10-1/2 oz. can beef broth
2 c. water
1/2 t. chili powder
1 t. sugar
1 t. salt
1/2 t. pepper

Combine ground beef, onion, celery and garlic over medium heat in a stockpot; cook until beef is browned and onion tender. Drain; stir in remaining ingredients. Reduce heat and simmer for 1-1/2 hours to blend flavors. Serves 8 to 10.

Oops! If a soup or stew begins to burn on the bottom,
all is not lost. Spoon it into another pan, being careful
not to scrape up the scorched food on the bottom.
The burnt taste usually won't linger.

Soups & Salads in a snap

Speedy Green Bean Salad

Angie Davis
Ainsworth, NE

A salad that's just a little different.

2 14-1/2 oz. cans French-style
   green beans
1 c. ranch salad dressing

4 T. bacon bits
2 T. onion, minced

Mix all ingredients together; refrigerate for 2 hours. Serves 6 to 8.

For a tasty addition to potato salad, try adding a jar of marinated artichoke hearts. Simply drain, chop and stir in along with the potatoes.

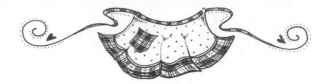

Super Seafood Chowder

Hilary Gibson-Blank
Montgomery City, MO

*A creamy soup that's good enough
for company...top with toasty croutons.*

1 onion, chopped
2 T. margarine
15-oz. can seafood chowder
2 c. half-and-half

3 potatoes, peeled and cubed
8-oz. pkg. frozen imitation
   crabmeat, thawed

In a large saucepan over medium heat, sauté onion in margarine until soft. Add chowder and half-and-half. Bring to a boil; add potatoes. Simmer over low heat until potatoes are cooked through. Add crabmeat; continue simmering until meat is warmed through. Serves 4 to 6.

Stir drained mandarin orange segments into sweet,
creamy coleslaw for a change of pace.

Greek Pasta Salad

Lisa Seymour
Blooming Prairie, MN

We love this hearty all-in-one dinner salad...all you need to add is some crusty bread sticks!

16-oz. pkg. rainbow rotini, uncooked
16-oz. pkg. frozen California-blend vegetables, cooked
16-oz. bottle Italian salad dressing
14-oz. can quartered artichoke hearts, drained

12-oz. pkg. sliced pepperoni
10-oz. pkg. crumbled feta cheese
4-oz. can black olives, drained and chopped
1/2 c. pesto
1 c. cherry tomatoes
1 red pepper, sliced

Cook rotini according to package directions; drain and rinse with cold water. Combine with vegetables in a large bowl. Toss with salad dressing; add remaining ingredients and mix well. Chill overnight; stir before serving. Makes 12 servings.

Save time when making a pasta dish that calls for frozen vegetables. Simply drop veggies into the boiling pasta pot in the last 5 minutes of cooking time...one less pot for clean-up!

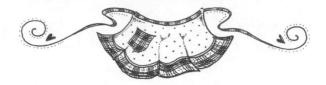

Red Bean Salad with Feta & Peppers

Kendall Hale
Lynn, MA

Just the thing to accompany juicy grilled burgers!

15-oz. can kidney beans,
   drained and rinsed
2 c. shredded cabbage
1 red pepper, chopped
2 green onions, chopped

1 c. crumbled feta cheese
1/3 c. fresh parsley, chopped
1 clove garlic, minced
2 to 3 T. lemon juice
1 to 2 T. olive oil

Combine all ingredients except lemon juice and olive oil in a large salad bowl. Add lemon juice and olive oil to taste; toss well. Cover and chill before serving. Serves 4.

Serve salad portions in red or yellow peppers, melon halves or tomato cups for a clever presentation...easy to serve on buffets too.

Antipasto Tortellini Salad

Doreen DeRosa
New Castle, PA

*It's great to pull this filling salad from the fridge after
an afternoon of shopping, gardening or just taking it easy!*

16-oz. pkg. cheese tortellini,
   uncooked
1/4 lb. salami, cubed
1/4 lb. provolone cheese,
   cut into strips
6-oz. jar marinated artichoke
   hearts, drained and sliced

6-oz. can black olives, drained,
   sliced and divided
1-1/2 c. Italian salad dressing
1/2 c. grated Parmesan cheese

Cook tortellini according to package directions; drain and rinse in
cold water. Combine tortellini, salami, provolone cheese, artichokes
and one cup olives in a large bowl; set aside. Combine salad dressing
and Parmesan cheese; pour over tortellini mixture and toss gently.
Top with remaining olives. Refrigerate one to 2 hours to blend flavors.
Makes 8 servings.

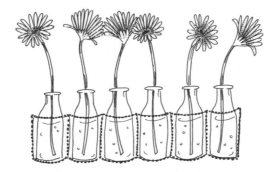

Serve a salad supper for a change of pace...try a pasta salad,
a chicken or tuna salad and a tossed salad.
Crusty, buttered bread and a simple dessert
complete the meal.

Aztec Corn Chowder

Vickie

I love this soup with all my favorite flavors!

1/4 c. butter
3-1/2 c. corn
1 clove garlic, minced
1 c. chicken broth
2 c. milk
1 t. dried oregano

4-oz. can diced green chiles
1 c. shredded Monterey
   Jack cheese
salt to taste
Optional: chopped tomato,
   chopped cilantro

Melt butter in a large saucepan over medium heat. Add corn and garlic; heat and stir until corn is heated through. Remove from heat. Place broth and 2 cups corn mixture into a blender. Cover and blend until smooth; stir into mixture in saucepan. Add milk, oregano and chiles and mix well; bring to a boil over medium heat, stirring constantly. Remove from heat; stir in cheese and salt to taste. Garnish with tomato and cilantro, if desired. Makes 4 to 6 servings.

Homemade savory crackers are a special touch for soup. Spread saltines with softened butter, then sprinkle with garlic salt, thyme, paprika or another favorite seasoning. Pop into a 350-degree oven just until golden, 3 to 6 minutes.

Chicken-Tortilla Soup

Mary Wade
Hutchinson, KS

*Top with a dollop of sour cream, crushed tortilla chips
and some chopped green onions.*

14-1/2 oz. can chicken broth
10-3/4 oz. can cream of
chicken soup
15-1/2 oz. can black beans,
drained and rinsed
14-oz. can sweet corn & diced
peppers, drained

10-oz. can tomatoes with chiles
12-oz. can chicken, drained
8-oz. pkg. pasteurized processed
cheese spread, diced

Combine all ingredients except cheese in a stockpot over medium-low
heat. When heated through, add cheese, stirring until melted.
Serves 6.

Need to feed a few extra guests? It's easy to stretch soup!
Some quick-cooking add-ins are orzo pasta, ramen noodles,
instant rice or canned beans. Simmer for just a
few minutes until heated through.

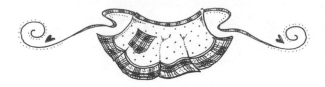

Nana's Cracker Salad

Karin Geach
Elk Grove, CA

An old-fashioned favorite.

1 sleeve saltine crackers,
   crushed
14-1/2 oz. can diced tomatoes,
   very well drained

1 egg, hard-boiled, peeled and
   finely chopped
3 green onions, finely chopped
1-1/2 c. mayonnaise

Mix all ingredients together; chill. To serve, scoop out lemon-size portions. Makes 6 servings.

Does your recipe call for cracker crumbs?
Seal crackers in a plastic zipping bag, then crush with
a rolling pin. No mess...this works well with cookies too!

Soups & Salads in a snap

Cape Cod Clam Chowder

Robin Cornett
Spring Hill, FL

*For smoky flavor, stir in some bacon that's been
crisply cooked and crumbled.*

2 10-3/4 oz. cans New England
   clam chowder
10-3/4 oz. can cream of
   celery soup
10-3/4 oz. can cream of
   potato soup
2 pts. half-and-half
3 potatoes, peeled and diced
salt and pepper to taste
Optional: chopped tomatoes,
   fresh chives

Combine soups and half-and-half in a large stockpot. Place over
medium-low heat until heated through, stirring often. Set aside over
low heat. Boil potatoes in water for about 10 minutes; drain and add
to soup mixture. Cook over medium heat until potatoes are tender.
Add salt and pepper to taste. Garnish with tomatoes and chives,
if desired. Serves 6 to 8.

Dress up a tube of refrigerated bread stick dough.
Before baking, brush the dough with a little beaten egg,
then sprinkle with sesame seed, grated Parmesan or
dried rosemary. A great accompaniment to soup!

Cowboy Stew

Andrea Pocreva
Navarre, FL

Try adding 2 ears of sweet corn, cut into one-inch lengths,
instead of the canned corn for a fun variation.

1 lb. ground beef
salt and pepper to taste
10-oz. can tomatoes with chiles
3 10-3/4 oz. cans minestrone
    soup

2 15-oz. cans ranch-style beans
15-1/4 oz. can corn
14-1/2 oz. can diced tomatoes

Brown ground beef in a stockpot; drain. Add salt and pepper to taste;
stir in remaining ingredients. Simmer over medium heat for
25 minutes, or until heated through. Serves 10.

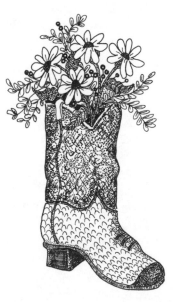

Crunchy tortilla strips are a tasty addition to
southwestern-style soups. Cut tortillas into strips,
then deep-fry quickly. Drain, then sprinkle on top of soup.

Scrumptious
Sides & Breads

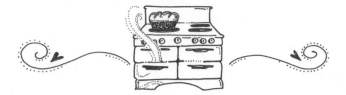

French Market Squash

Beth Boyd
Atlanta, TX

A luscious way to serve your garden's summer bounty of squash.

2 lbs. yellow squash, cubed
8-oz. container sour cream
10-3/4 oz. can cream of
    chicken soup
1 onion, chopped

6-oz. pkg. herb-flavored stuffing
    mix, divided
1/2 c. butter, melted
1 t. salt
1/2 t. pepper

Place squash in a saucepan and cover with water; simmer over medium heat until nearly tender. Drain. Mix squash, sour cream, soup, onion, half the stuffing mix, butter, salt and pepper. Spoon into a greased 13"x9" baking pan; sprinkle with remaining stuffing mix. Bake at 350 degrees for 45 minutes. Serves 8.

A fun new way to serve cornbread...mix up the batter, thin slightly with a little extra milk, then bake until crisp in a waffle iron.

Scrumptious Sides & Breads

Tomato-Basil Cheese Pie

Barb Mitchusson
Poulsbo, WA

This savory pie makes a delicious light lunch or supper.

8-oz. pkg. shredded mozzarella
   cheese, divided
9-inch pie crust
4 tomatoes, chopped
1 c. fresh basil, chopped

4 cloves garlic, minced
1/2 c. mayonnaise
1/4 c. grated Parmesan cheese
1/8 t. white pepper
Garnish: fresh basil

Sprinkle 1/2 cup mozzarella cheese into pie crust. Top with tomatoes
and set aside. Combine basil and garlic; sprinkle over tomatoes. Set
aside. Mix remaining mozzarella cheese, mayonnaise, Parmesan
cheese and pepper together; spread over basil mixture. Bake at
375 degrees for 35 to 40 minutes, or until golden. Garnish with a few
leaves of basil. Serves 6 to 8.

A fresh garnish really makes food look tastier.
Try tucking herb sprigs, carrot curls or cherry tomatoes
around the edge for a contrast in color and texture.

Cheesy Vegetable Casserole

Colleen McAleavey
Plum, PA

We like to vary this casserole by choosing
different blends of frozen vegetables.

2 16-oz. pkgs. frozen stir-fry
   blend vegetables, thawed
   and drained
16-oz. pkg. pasteurized
   processed cheese spread

1/4 c. milk
1/2 c. butter
1 sleeve buttery round
   crackers, crushed

Place vegetables in a lightly greased 13"x9" baking pan; set aside.
Melt cheese spread in a saucepan; add milk. Stir over low heat until
smooth; pour over vegetables. Melt butter and stir in cracker crumbs;
sprinkle over vegetables. Bake at 350 degrees, uncovered, for 20 to
25 minutes. Makes 6 to 8 servings.

To thaw frozen veggies quickly, place them in a colander
and pour boiling water over to separate. Finish cooking in
baked dishes like casseroles or on the stovetop as a side.

Scrumptious Sides & Breads

Crescent Chive Rolls

Kerry Mayer
Dunham Springs, LA

Warm rolls, fragrant with the mild oniony taste of chives.

8-oz. tube refrigerated
   crescent rolls

1 T. butter, melted
1/4 c. fresh chives, chopped

Unroll dough; brush one side with butter. Divide dough into triangles.
Sprinkle buttered side of each triangle with chives and roll into
crescent shape. Arrange on an ungreased baking sheet. Bake at
375 degrees for 10 to 13 minutes, or until golden. Immediately
remove from baking sheet; serve warm. Makes 8 rolls.

Keep a pot of chives on a sunny kitchen windowsill for
fresh-picked flavor year 'round...just snip off
a blade or 2 as needed for a recipe or garnish.

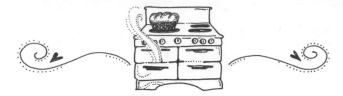

Those Potatoes

Teri Peterson
Thornton, CO

*Every time there's a party everyone asks,
"Are you going to make those potatoes?"*

32-oz. pkg. frozen onion-
   flavored potato puffs
1/2 c. margarine
10-3/4 oz. can cream of
   chicken soup

8-oz. container sour cream
1 bunch green onions, chopped
8-oz. pkg. shredded Cheddar
   cheese, divided

Place potato puffs in a lightly greased 11"x9" baking pan; set aside.
Melt butter in a saucepan; add soup, sour cream, onions and one cup
cheese. Stir over low heat until mixed; pour over potatoes. Sprinkle
remaining cheese over top. Bake for 30 minutes at 350 degrees.
Makes 6 to 8 servings.

Potluck dinners are a wonderful way to share
food and fellowship with friends. Why not make a
standing date once a month to try new recipes
as well as tried & true favorites?

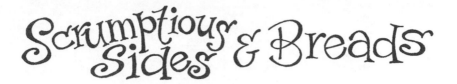

Slow-Cooker Stuffing Balls

Pam Granger
Moscow, Russia

We love stuffing...this is an easy way to fix it without the turkey!

2 c. chicken-flavored
    stuffing mix
2 eggs, beaten
14-3/4 oz. can creamed corn
1/2 c. onion, chopped

1/2 c. celery, chopped
1/4 c. water
1 t. poultry seasoning
pepper to taste
1/4 c. butter, melted

Combine all ingredients except butter in a medium bowl; mix well.
Shape into balls in whatever size you prefer. Arrange stuffing balls in a
slow cooker; drizzle with melted butter. Cover and cook on low setting
for 3-1/2 to 4 hours. Serves 8 to 10.

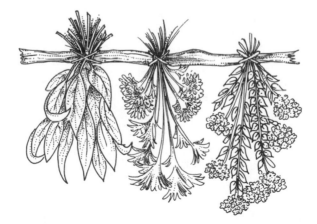

Ensure flavorful herbs for cooking...use a felt-tip pen
to mark the date on newly purchased jars.
Dried herbs will stay fresh for about 6 months.

Savory Herb-Roasted Veggies

Jo Ann

Let the season dictate your choice of veggies...red and yellow peppers, zucchini, asparagus and sweet onions in summer, sweet potatoes, carrots, beets and parsnips in winter.

5 c. assorted vegetables, peeled
   and thickly sliced or cubed

1/3 c. Italian salad dressing
1/3 c. grated Parmesan cheese

Toss all ingredients together in a large bowl to coat vegetables.
Place in a lightly greased, aluminum foil-lined jelly-roll pan.
Grill over medium heat or bake at 450 degrees, stirring occasionally,
for 40 to 45 minutes, or until vegetables are tender. Serves 6.

If a recipe calls for a crunchy crumb topping,
there are lots of choices besides bread crumbs.
Crushed potato chips, savory snack crackers,
pretzels or corn flake cereal are all worth a try.

Scrumptious Sides & Breads

Rustic Potatoes

Kristina Camacho
Willow Grove, PA

*The topping of crispy bacon and chopped olives
makes this potato casserole look as good as it tastes.*

12 to 14 potatoes,
   peeled and cubed
1 c. mayonnaise
1 onion, diced
1/2 c. green pepper, diced
3/4 lb. shredded sharp
   Cheddar cheese

salt and pepper to taste
1/2 lb. bacon, crisply cooked
   and crumbled
1/2 c. green olives, chopped

Cover potatoes with water in a saucepan; boil for 10 minutes, until partially cooked through. Drain. Combine potatoes, mayonnaise, onion, green pepper, cheese, salt and pepper in a large bowl; mix well. Place in a greased 13"x9" baking pan; top with bacon and olives. Bake at 325 degrees, uncovered, for one hour, or until potatoes are tender and golden. Serves 12 to 14.

Baked tomatoes are a tasty garnish for grilled meats.
Cut ripe tomatoes in half, dot with butter, then sprinkle with
grated Parmesan cheese and oregano. Bake at
425 degrees for 10 to 15 minutes.

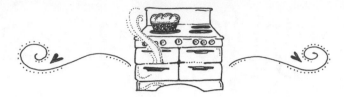

Best-Ever Cornbread

Sherry Shell
Lumberton, TX

It's easy to double this recipe...bake in a 13"x9" baking pan.

7-oz. pkg. cornbread mix
2 eggs
1/4 c. oil

1 c. sour cream
1 c. creamed corn
Optional: diced jalapeños to taste

Mix all ingredients together in a medium bowl. Pour into a lightly greased 8" round baking pan. Bake at 400 degrees for 35 minutes, or until golden. Serves 6 to 8.

Sweet, little servings of butter are easy to make with a melon baller...a charming change from butter pats.
Or press butter into decorative candy molds,
then chill and pop out.

Scrumptious Sides & Breads

Crispy Fried Zucchini

Staci Meyers
Cocoa, FL

*Sometimes I like to use a mixture of grated Parmesan,
Romano and asiago cheeses in this recipe.*

1 c. Italian-seasoned dry
   bread crumbs
1/2 c. grated Parmesan cheese
salt and pepper to taste
2 to 4 zucchini, cut into
   slices or strips

2 eggs, beaten
oil for frying
Garnish: marinara sauce,
   horseradish sauce

Combine crumbs, cheese, salt and pepper in a bowl; set aside. Dip
zucchini into beaten egg, then into crumb mixture to coat evenly. Heat
oil in a skillet; fry zucchini a few at a time until tender and golden.
Serve with sauces for dipping. Makes 6 to 8 servings.

Batter-fried veggies will be crispier if they're patted dry
before being dipped into batter.

Sweet Corn & Rice Casserole

Linda Stone
Cookeville, TN

Roll up leftovers in a flour tortilla for a hearty snack.

2 T. butter
1 green pepper, chopped
1 onion, chopped
15-1/2 oz. can creamed corn
11-oz. can sweet corn & diced
    peppers, drained
11-oz. can corn, drained
6 c. prepared rice

10-oz. can tomatoes with chiles
8-oz. pkg. mild Mexican
    pasteurized processed cheese
    spread, cubed
1/2 t. salt
1/4 t. pepper
1/2 c. shredded Cheddar cheese

Melt butter in a large skillet over medium heat. Add green pepper and onion; sauté 5 minutes, or until tender. Stir in remaining ingredients except shredded cheese; spoon into a lightly greased 13"x9" baking pan. Bake at 350 degrees for 25 to 30 minutes, until heated through. Top with shredded cheese; bake an additional 5 minutes, until cheese melts. Makes 10 to 12 servings.

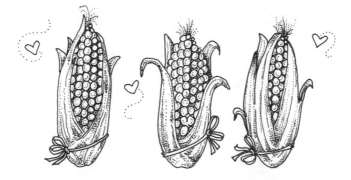

Keep a couple of favorite side dishes on hand in the freezer to make spur-of-the-moment entertaining easy. Pair them with grilled meats or a deli roast chicken for a hearty meal.

Broccoli Cornbread

Cathy Jackson
Iona, ID

Yummy at dinner…good as an appetizer too!

1/2 c. butter, melted
1 onion, chopped
10-oz. pkg. frozen broccoli,
　cooked and drained
4 eggs, beaten

1/4 c. buttermilk
8-oz. pkg. shredded
　Cheddar cheese
7-oz. pkg. cornbread mix

Pour melted butter into a bowl; add onion, broccoli, eggs, buttermilk and cheese. Mix well; stir in cornbread mix. Spoon into a greased 13"x9" baking pan; bake at 375 degrees for 25 to 30 minutes. Serves 12 to 14.

Don't have a biscuit cutter handy? Use the open end of a clean, empty soup can to cut biscuit dough.

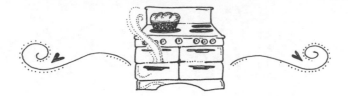

Fantastic Fried Rice

Denise Blaine
Sheppard AFB, TX

A terrific side dish for grilled chicken, or add a little more ham to create a delicious main dish.

1/2 c. cooked ham, diced
1 onion, chopped
2 T. oil
4-oz. can sliced mushrooms,
  drained

4 c. prepared rice
1 c. frozen mixed vegetables
1/4 c. soy sauce
2 eggs, beaten

Over medium heat, sauté ham and onion in oil in a wok or large skillet until lightly browned. Add mushrooms, rice and vegetables and heat until vegetables are tender; add soy sauce. Make a hole in the center of mixture; reduce heat. Add eggs and stir until eggs are completely cooked, about 5 minutes. Serves 6 to 8.

Try tiny orzo pasta in place of rice for a delicious change in favorite recipes.

Scrumptious Sides & Breads

Spicy Sesame Noodles

Kathy Ward
Great Falls, MT

We love this quick-to-make noodle dish! It's best served right away.

10 c. water
5 3-oz. pkgs. ramen noodles
2 cloves garlic
1/2 c. oil

1/4 c. soy sauce
2 t. sesame oil
2 t. red pepper flakes
2 T. sesame seed

Bring water to a boil in a large stockpot. Add noodles (reserving seasoning packets for another recipe) and garlic; boil for 3 minutes. Drain well and discard garlic; mix in remaining ingredients. Serve immediately. Makes 10 servings.

You're never too old for party favors! Send your guests home with a whimsical memento...tiny potted plants, little bags of homemade candy, mini photo frames or even jars of bubble-blowing liquid!

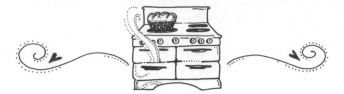

Company Creamed Spinach

Zana Shults
Marlton, NJ

Stir in a little chopped fresh basil or dill for a special flavor.

10-oz. pkg. frozen chopped
   spinach
1 T. dried, minced onion

1-1/2 T. bacon bits
1/2 to 3/4 c. sour cream

Prepare spinach according to package directions; add onion and bacon bits to cooking water halfway through cooking time. Drain well; stir in sour cream to desired consistency. Makes 4 servings.

Make a scrumptious topping for veggies using leftover bread or rolls. Sauté soft bread crumbs in olive oil or butter until golden...sprinkle with dried herbs for extra flavor.

Ripe Tomato Tart

Darlene Lohrman
Chicago, IL

Fresh roma tomatoes are available year 'round
so you can enjoy this summery-tasting pie anytime.

9-inch pie crust
1-1/2 c. shredded mozzarella
    cheese, divided
4 roma tomatoes,
    cut into wedges

3/4 c. fresh basil, chopped
4 cloves garlic, minced
1/2 c. mayonnaise
1/2 c. grated Parmesan cheese
1/8 t. white pepper

Line an ungreased 9" tart pan with pie crust; press crust into fluted sides of pan and trim edges. Bake at 450 degrees for 5 to 7 minutes; remove from oven. Sprinkle with 1/2 cup mozzarella cheese; let cool on a wire rack. Combine remaining ingredients; mix well and fill crust. Reduce heat to 375 degrees; bake for about 20 minutes, or until bubbly on top. Makes 6 servings.

Light a welcoming path for guests...wind twinkling mini lights along the walk to your front door.

Crispy Onion Potatoes

Janet Smith
Woodland Hills, CA

Fines herbes is a classic blend of thyme, marjoram, oregano, parsley and other dried herbs. Substitute just one or 2 of these if you prefer...the result will be equally tasty.

1-1/2 oz. pkg. onion soup mix
1/2 c. olive oil
1/4 c. butter, melted
1 t. fines herbes
1/4 t. pepper
2 lbs. potatoes, quartered
Optional: fresh parsley, chopped

Blend soup mix, oil, butter, herbs and pepper together in an ungreased 13"x9" baking pan. Add potatoes; stir to coat. Bake at 400 degrees for one hour, or until potatoes are tender and golden. Sprinkle with parsley, if desired. Serves 6 to 8.

Set out a guest book when guests come to dinner! They'll feel honored to sign it and you'll have a special memento. Include the menu served too...it'll make planning future dinners easier.

Scrumptious Sides & Breads

Yummy Garden Bread

Cara Killingsworth
Shamrock, TX

A savory version of the popular Monkey Bread.

2 12-oz. tubes refrigerated
   biscuits
5 slices bacon, crisply cooked
   and crumbled

1/4 c. green pepper, chopped
1/4 c. onion, chopped
1/2 c. shredded Cheddar cheese
1/2 c. margarine, melted

Quarter biscuits and set aside. Combine remaining ingredients; toss
with biscuits to coat. Pour into an ungreased Bundt® pan; bake at
350 degrees for 30 minutes. Invert onto a platter and serve hot.
Makes 8 to 10 servings.

Stir diced, sautéed mushrooms, onions or celery into
prepared wild rice mix for a homemade touch.

Super Slow-Cooker Beans

Brenda St. Thomas
St. Leonard, MD

A snap to fix...the slow cooker does all the work!

1 onion, chopped
1/2 c. cider vinegar
1 c. brown sugar, packed
1 t. dry mustard
16-oz. can lima beans, drained

15-1/2 oz. can kidney beans, drained
16-oz. can butter beans, drained
2 15-oz. cans pork & beans

Combine onion, vinegar, sugar and mustard in a slow cooker; cover and cook on high setting for one hour. Add remaining ingredients; cover and cook on low setting for 6 to 8 hours. Serves 8 to 10.

A centerpiece in a snap...arrange 3 pillar candles of different heights on a plate, then wind with tiny tinsel garland or tuck fresh flowers around the base.

Cheddar-Parmesan Bread

Krista Starnes
Middletown, RI

This bread is so easy to make and I always have the ingredients in my pantry. It smells like pizza while it's baking...heavenly!

1-1/2 c. biscuit baking mix
1 c. shredded Cheddar cheese
1/4 c. grated Parmesan cheese
1/2 t. dried oregano
1/2 c. milk

1 egg, beaten
2 T. butter, melted
Garnish: grated Parmesan
   cheese

Mix first 6 ingredients in a bowl; stir together to form a thick batter. Spoon into a greased 8" round cake pan. Drizzle with melted butter; sprinkle with additional Parmesan cheese. Bake at 400 degrees for 20 minutes, or until a toothpick inserted in the center comes out clean. Let cool for 10 minutes; cut into wedges and serve warm. Makes 6 to 8 servings.

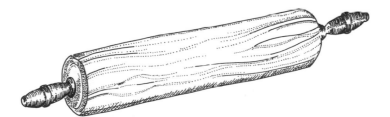

No-fuss thawing...simply move frozen dishes to the fridge early the day before.

Melodee's Mushroom Medley

Kimberlee Schmidgall
Tremont, IL

*My sister Melodee's creation...use any combination
of mushrooms you like.*

1 onion, chopped
1 c. butter
14-oz. pkg. herb-flavored
   stuffing mix
3 c. button mushrooms, sliced
3 c. portabella mushrooms,
   sliced
3 c. morel mushrooms, sliced

salt and pepper to taste
dried parsley to taste
10-3/4 oz. can cream of
   mushroom soup
2/3 c. milk
1 egg, beaten
3 c. shredded Cheddar cheese

Sauté onion in butter until transparent; combine with stuffing mix
in a medium bowl. Spoon half of mixture into a 13"x9" baking pan
sprayed with non-stick vegetable spray; set aside. Combine all
mushrooms and seasonings in a large bowl; mix well and spoon over
stuffing mixture. Combine soup and milk in a small bowl, mixing well;
stir in beaten egg. Pour over mushrooms; top with cheese, then with
remaining stuffing mixture. Bake at 350 degrees for 40 minutes,
or until golden. Let stand 5 minutes before serving. Makes 6 to
8 servings.

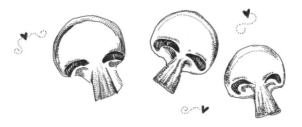

Fringe a square of homespun...a quick & easy liner
for a basket of warm muffins.

Orange-Glazed Carrots

Staci Meyers
Cocoa, FL

Add a spoonful of orange marmalade or apricot jam...the kids will be happy to eat their veggies tonight!

16-oz. pkg. baby carrots
1/2 c. orange juice
5 T. brown sugar, packed

2 T. butter
1/8 t. salt

Place carrots in a medium saucepan. Cover with water and boil until tender; drain and return to saucepan. Add orange juice to saucepan; simmer until juice is nearly evaporated. Stir in remaining ingredients; heat until butter is melted and mixture is well blended. Serves 4 to 6.

A crock of honey butter is tasty at any meal. Simply combine 1/2 cup softened butter with 2/3 cup honey, using an electric mixer on low speed.

Green Chile-Rice Casserole

Kathy Grashoff
Fort Wayne, IN

A quick & easy Mexican favorite.

3 c. prepared rice
16-oz. container sour cream
1/8 t. salt
1-1/2 c. shredded Monterey
    Jack cheese

4 4-oz. cans chopped
    green chiles
1/2 c. shredded Colby cheese

Combine rice, sour cream and salt; spoon half of mixture into a greased 13"x9" baking pan. Sprinkle with Monterey Jack cheese; top with green chiles. Spread remaining rice mixture over the top; sprinkle with Colby cheese. Bake at 350 degrees for 30 minutes. Serves 6 to 8.

Stuffed tomatoes or summer squash are a delicious way
to serve rice or dressing! Scoop out the pulp and prebake for
10 minutes at 350 degrees, then fill and bake for an
additional 10 minutes, until hot. Sprinkle with herbs
or grated cheese, if you like.

Slow-Cooker 5-Bean Casserole

Kim Smith
Greensburg, PA

Sausage makes this extra hearty.

14-1/2 oz. can green beans,
   drained
16-oz. can lima beans, drained
16-oz. can pork & beans
16-oz. can black beans
15-1/2 oz. can chili beans
10-3/4 oz. can tomato soup
6-oz. can tomato paste
1 c. barbecue sauce
1 c. brown sugar, packed
1 lb. ground mild or hot
   sausage, browned
   and drained

Combine beans in a slow cooker; set aside. Mix together remaining ingredients; stir into beans. Cover and cook on high setting for 3 to 4 hours. Makes 10 to 12 servings.

Did you know bread will stay freshest if it's stored on the counter, not refrigerated. Or drop it into a freezer bag and freeze for up to a month. Pop a frozen slice or 2 into the toaster for immediate use or let it thaw at room temperature.

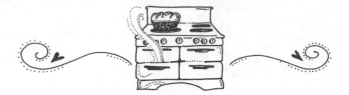

Great Italian Garlic Bread

Angela DeFrancisco
Millville, NJ

No spaghetti dinner would be complete without this!

1 loaf Italian bread, sliced in half
   lengthwise
3 to 4 cloves garlic, minced

1/2 c. butter, softened
Garnish: grated Parmesan
   cheese, dried parsley

Place bread on an ungreased baking sheet; set aside. Combine garlic and butter; mix well. Spread over cut side of bread; sprinkle with Parmesan cheese and parsley. Bake at 425 degrees for 5 to 10 minutes. Slice and serve warm. Serves 6 to 8.

Onion French Bread

Connie McGuire
Madras, OR

A delicious accompaniment to soups & stews.

1 loaf French bread, sliced in
   half lengthwise
1 c. mayonnaise

1/2 c. onion, chopped
1/2 c. grated Parmesan cheese
Garnish: paprika

Place bread on an ungreased baking sheet and set aside. Mix mayonnaise, onion and cheese; spread over cut side of bread. Sprinkle with paprika; broil for 3 to 5 minutes, or until golden. Slice and serve warm. Serves 6 to 8.

Oops! You forgot to set out a cold stick of butter to soften. No problem...use a hand grater to shred the butter into little pieces. It will soften quickly.

Farmers' Market Pie

Evelyn Yearty
Gulf Hammock, FL

Can be served as either a savory side or a meatless main dish.

10-inch pie crust
1/2 to 1 lb. sliced mushrooms
1 onion, sliced
2 to 3 zucchini, sliced
1 green pepper, sliced

4 T. butter
1 tomato, sliced
salt and pepper to taste
1 c. mayonnaise
1 c. shredded mozzarella cheese

Prebake crust in an ungreased pie plate at 350 degrees for 20 minutes; set aside. Sauté mushrooms, onion, zucchini and green pepper in butter over medium heat. Arrange tomato slices in the bottom of pie crust; top with sautéed vegetables. Sprinkle with salt and pepper; set aside. Combine mayonnaise and cheese; spread over vegetables. Bake at 350 degrees for 35 minutes, or until golden. Serves 8 to 10.

Add a personal touch to refrigerated biscuits...brush with butter, then sprinkle with coarse salt or sesame, caraway or poppy seed before baking.

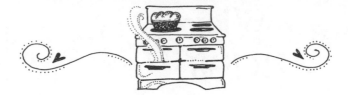

Easy Cheesy Parmesan Bread

Denise Hazen
Cincinnati, OH

*Add a teaspoon or 2 of minced garlic to the butter
to make garlic Parmesan bread.*

2 10-oz. tubes refrigerated
   biscuits

1 c. butter, melted
1 c. shredded Parmesan cheese

Dip each biscuit in butter; roll in cheese. Place in a greased and floured Bundt® pan; drizzle with remaining butter. Bake at 375 degrees for 25 to 30 minutes, or until golden. Turn out of pan while still warm. Serves 8 to 10.

Keep freshly baked bread warm & toasty...simply slip a piece
of aluminum foil into the bread basket,
then top it with a decorative napkin or tea towel.

Scrumptious Sides & Breads

Jean's Savory Succotash

Jean Pasley
Hanford, CA

Even better made with fresh sweet corn! Simply combine the kernels cut from 4 ears of corn with a small box of frozen baby lima beans.

16-oz. pkg. frozen succotash
3/4 c. water
1/4 c. butter
1 onion, chopped

1 T. dried parsley
1 t. coarse salt
1/2 t. pepper

Combine succotash and water in a saucepan; set aside. In a small skillet, melt butter and sauté onion over medium heat until transparent. Add onion to succotash along with remaining ingredients. Simmer over medium-low heat for 30 minutes, until tender. Makes 4 to 6 servings.

Try using canned chicken broth in place of water when cooking pasta or vegetables...you'll be surprised how much flavor it adds!

Super-Easy Corn Casserole

Lisa Brown
Groves, TX

Warm and filling…real comfort food!

14-3/4 oz. can creamed corn
15-oz. can corn, drained
6-oz. pkg. chicken-flavored
   stuffing mix
8-oz. pkg. shredded sharp
   Cheddar cheese

2 eggs, beaten
1 onion, grated
1 green pepper, chopped
2-oz. jar diced pimentos, drained
1/2 c. margarine, melted
1 T. sugar

Mix all ingredients together; spoon into a greased 13"x9" baking pan.
Bake at 350 degrees for 45 to 55 minutes; let stand 5 minutes before
serving. Serves 6 to 8.

Hosting a party? All kinds of colorful, fun items for
table decorating, serving and party favors are
as near as your neighborhood dollar store!

Stuffed Pumpernickel Bread

Bernadette Reed
Berlin Heights, OH

This is absolutely one of our family's favorites...the warm cheese filling is irresistible!

1 loaf pumpernickel bread
1-1/2 c. shredded Swiss cheese
1 c. mayonnaise
1 t. garlic powder

1/2 t. dried parsley
1/2 t. dried basil
1/2 t. dried oregano
1/2 t. dried thyme

Slice bread into serving-size slices, but do not cut all the way through the bottom crust; set aside. Mix remaining ingredients together; spoon mixture between slices of bread. Wrap loaf in aluminum foil; sprinkle with a few drops of water and seal tightly. Bake at 350 degrees for 30 minutes, or until cheese is melted. Serves 6 to 8.

Herb butter is scrumptious on warm bread!
Blend together softened butter and chopped fresh herbs
like chives or marjoram. Add a touch of lemon juice if you like.
Roll up in wax paper and chill, then slice to serve.

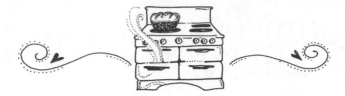

Wild Rice Bake

Cindy Bland
El Dorado Springs, MO

A wonderful casserole to fix and forget...slip it into the oven alongside a roast.

2 10-1/2 oz. cans beef broth
2 10-3/4 oz. cans French
    onion soup
1 c. butter, diced
2 8-oz. cans sliced water
    chestnuts, drained

8-oz. can sliced mushrooms,
    drained
6-oz. pkg. long grain and wild
    rice with seasoning packet,
    uncooked

Mix all ingredients in an ungreased 13"x9" baking pan. Cover and bake for one hour at 350 degrees. Serves 6 to 8.

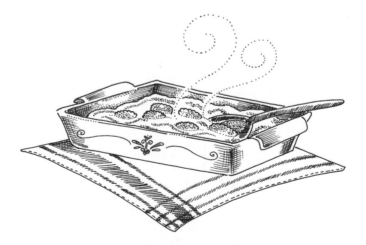

Food should be prepared with butter and love.

-Swedish Proverb

Scrumptious Sides & Breads

Bacon-Mushroom Casserole

Charlotte Mayes
Carmel, IN

*It's easy to prepare and so good! Sometimes I add chopped
green and red peppers for a festive look.*

6-oz. pkg. garlic & onion
   croutons
4-oz. can sliced mushrooms,
   drained
2-oz. jar bacon bits

8-oz. pkg. shredded Colby
   & Monterey Jack cheese
7 eggs
1-3/4 c. half-and-half
salt-free seasoning to taste

Layer croutons, mushrooms, bacon bits and cheese in a greased
13"x9" baking pan; set aside. Whisk together eggs and half-and-half
in a medium bowl; pour over top. Sprinkle to taste with salt-free
seasoning. Cover and refrigerate overnight. Bake, uncovered, at
350 degrees for 30 to 35 minutes, or until a knife inserted in the
center comes out clean. Let stand 5 minutes before serving.
Makes 12 servings.

Tie rolled-up napkins with several strands of jute and slip in
a single blossom...simple and charming!

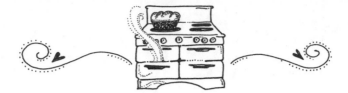

Crescent Herb Swirls

Tiffany Brinkley
Broomfield, CO

Adjust seasonings to taste, just the way your family likes them.

2 T. olive oil
1 t. Italian seasoning
1/4 t. onion powder
1/4 t. garlic powder
2 8-oz. tubes refrigerated
   crescent rolls

Combine oil and seasonings in a small bowl; mix well. Unroll one tube of dough on a very lightly floured surface. Press perforations firmly to seal and form a 13-inch by 7-inch rectangle. Brush with oil mixture. Unroll second tube of dough; press perforations to seal. Place over herb filling; seal dough edges. Cut dough lengthwise into 8 strips. Twist each strip 5 to 6 times; shape each one into a coil. Place in 8 greased muffin cups. Bake at 375 degrees for 15 to 20 minutes, or until golden. Remove immediately from pan; serve warm. Makes 8 rolls.

Give breads and pastries a beautiful finish. Whisk together a tablespoon of water with an egg yolk for a golden finish, or an egg white for a shiny luster. Brush over bread just before baking...so easy!

Spinach-Noodle Bake

Dorothy Lester
Hickory Hills, IL

A potluck favorite.

3 eggs
8-oz. container cottage cheese
8-oz. container sour cream
2 10-oz. pkgs. frozen chopped
   spinach, thawed and drained

16-oz. pkg. spinach egg noodles,
   cooked
salt and pepper to taste
3/4 c. shredded Cheddar cheese

Beat eggs and cottage cheese together; stir in sour cream. Set aside.
Combine spinach and prepared noodles; add egg mixture. Sprinkle
with salt and pepper; pour into a greased 13"x9" baking pan. Top with
cheese; bake at 350 degrees for 40 minutes. Serves 10 to 12.

Decorative candles will burn longer when stored
in the refrigerator before lighting.

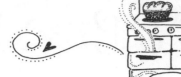

Dilly Sour Cream Bread

Bec Popovich
Gooseberry Patch

*A savory home-baked bread...stores well in the fridge
for up to 10 days.*

3 c. biscuit baking mix
1-1/4 c. shredded Cheddar
   cheese
3/4 c. milk
1/2 c. sour cream

1 egg, beaten
1 T. sugar
3/4 t. dill weed
3/4 t. dry mustard

Combine all ingredients in a mixing bowl; stir just until moistened.
Pour into a well-greased 9"x5" loaf pan. Bake at 350 degrees for
45 to 50 minutes, until golden. Let cool in pan 5 minutes. Remove
from pan and cool completely on a wire rack for 2 hours before slicing.
Store tightly wrapped. Makes one loaf.

When baking in dark non-stick baking pans, set the oven
temperature 25 degrees lower...baked goods won't overbrown.

Supper Shortcuts

Crispy Pecan-Crusted Chicken

Jo Ann

Cut the chicken into strips to make fun-to-eat chicken fingers.

4 boneless, skinless chicken breasts	1 c. ranch salad dressing 3 c. pecans, finely chopped

In a large plastic zipping bag, toss chicken with salad dressing to coat. Seal bag; refrigerate for one hour to overnight. Remove chicken from dressing; roll each in pecans until well-coated. Arrange chicken in a single layer in a lightly greased 13"x9" baking pan. Bake at 450 degrees for 20 to 25 minutes, until chicken juices run clear and pecans are crisp and golden. Makes 4 servings.

Shallow baskets make lunch or dinner fun! Just line with
a bright-colored paper napkin and fill with finger foods
like corn dogs, chicken nuggets and French fries.
Pass some extra napkins...no utensils required!

Supper Shortcuts

Baked Chicken & Rice

Gale Crayton
Clearwater, FL

*Almost a meal in itself...just add a side of steamed,
buttered broccoli and a basket of fresh-baked rolls.*

1 c. instant rice, uncooked
10-3/4 oz. can cream of
   chicken soup
1/2 c. water

2 T. butter, diced
salt and pepper to taste
2 boneless, skinless chicken
   breasts, cut into strips

Mix rice, soup and water; place in a lightly greased 8"x8" baking pan.
Dot with butter, salt and pepper; arrange chicken on top. Cover with
aluminum foil and bake at 350 degrees for 45 minutes; uncover and
bake an additional 10 minutes, until chicken is tender. Serves 2 to 4.

Sprinkle chopped herbs around the edge of dinner plates
to make a scrumptious meal look even yummier.

Pizza Potato Puff Casserole

Gladys Kielar
Perrysburg, OH

Friday night is pizza night at our house...sometimes our family enjoys this pizza for variety.

1 lb. ground beef
1/4 c. onion, chopped
10-3/4 oz. can cream of
    mushroom soup
8-oz. can pizza sauce

12 to 15 slices pepperoni
1/2 c. green pepper, chopped
1 c. shredded mozzarella cheese
16-oz. pkg. frozen potato puffs

In a large skillet, cook ground beef and onion over medium-high heat until browned, stirring frequently. Drain. Spoon beef mixture into an 8"x8" baking pan lightly sprayed with non-stick vegetable spray. Spoon pizza sauce evenly over beef; arrange pepperoni and green pepper over sauce. Sprinkle with cheese; arrange potato puffs over top. Cover with aluminum foil; bake at 375 degrees for 30 minutes. Uncover; bake an additional 15 to 20 minutes, until heated through. Serves 4.

An edible centerpiece is so easy! Simply pile colorful fruit
in a basket, then tuck nuts into the spaces in between.
We like lemons and almonds in summer,
apples and walnuts in fall.

Supper Shortcuts

Easy Cheesy Lasagna

Amy Blanchard
Hazel Park, MI

All the flavor of traditional lasagna...none of the effort.

1/2 lb. ground beef
26-oz. jar spaghetti sauce
8-oz. pkg. wide egg noodles,
   cooked

8-oz. pkg. shredded mozzarella
   cheese
1 c. cottage cheese
1 c. grated Parmesan cheese

Brown ground beef in a saucepan; drain. Stir sauce into beef; simmer for 5 minutes. Add noodles, mozzarella cheese and cottage cheese; stir together and place in a greased 2-quart casserole dish. Sprinkle with Parmesan cheese; bake at 350 degrees for 30 minutes. Serves 4 to 6.

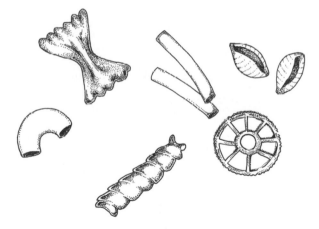

Try a different pasta shape in your favorite recipe.
Short shapes like shells, spirals, penne and bows
are great in casseroles.

Shelly's Pork Chops & Rice

Michele Billingsley
Boerne, TX

*This is my family's favorite comfort food.
If we haven't had it for awhile, they start asking for it!*

4 to 6 pork chops
1 T. oil
10-3/4 oz. can cream of
   mushroom soup

4-oz. can sliced mushrooms,
   drained and liquid reserved
2 c. long-cooking rice, uncooked

Brown pork chops lightly in oil in a skillet; drain and set aside. Combine soup, reserved liquid from mushrooms and enough water to equal 3 cups; mix well and pour into skillet. Stir in mushrooms and rice; top with pork chops. Cover and simmer for 30 to 45 minutes, or until rice is tender. Serves 4 to 6.

Pick up a bundle of fresh flowers when you shop for groceries.
Tucked into a pitcher or glass jar, even humble daisies
are charming and cheerful!

Supper Shortcuts

Jambalaya

Patricia Perkins
Shenandoah, IA

Add a little more hot pepper sauce if you like it spicy!

2 T. butter
7-oz. pkg. chicken-flavored rice
   vermicelli mix
2-3/4 c. water
1/4 t. pepper
1/4 t. hot pepper sauce

1 T. dried, minced onion
1/4 c. celery, diced
1/4 c. green pepper, diced
2 c. cooked ham, diced
1 lb. cooked, peeled
   medium shrimp

Melt butter in a large saucepan over medium heat. Add rice vermicelli mix and sauté just until golden. Stir in remaining ingredients; reduce heat, cover and simmer for 15 minutes. Serves 4 to 6.

Hot! Hot! If a dish turns out spicier than you expected, turn down the heat by stirring in a tablespoon each of sugar and lemon or lime juice.

Oven Beef & Noodles

Kristie Rigo
Friedens, PA

I like to make this stick-to-your-ribs dish on cold winter days.

1-1/2 oz. pkg. onion soup mix
4 c. water
10-3/4 oz. can cream of
    mushroom soup

3-lb. boneless beef chuck roast
12-oz. pkg. kluski egg noodles,
    uncooked
2 T. dried parsley

Combine onion soup mix and water in a covered roasting pan; stir in mushroom soup. Place roast in pan on top of soup mixture. Cover and bake at 350 degrees for 4 hours, or until meat is very tender. Remove roast from pan and shred; return to pan. Add noodles to pan; reduce heat to 300 degrees and bake for 20 to 30 minutes, checking and stirring every 15 minutes until noodles are tender. Add water if necessary to prevent drying out. Sprinkle with parsley before serving. Makes 6 to 8 servings.

Make any dinner table more welcoming with a pretty tablecloth. Don't hesitate to use the lace tablecloth you've tucked away or look for interesting yard goods at the fabric store.

Supper Shortcuts

Cheesy Chicken Pot Pie

Jana Warnell
Kalispell, MT

*I was always on the lookout for a good chicken pot pie...finally
I found this one in a cookbook for kids. Now it's a family staple!*

2 9-inch pie crusts
2 10-3/4 oz. cans cream of
   potato soup
2 c. cooked chicken, cubed

15-oz. can mixed vegetables,
   drained
2 c. shredded Cheddar cheese

Line an ungreased 9" pie plate with one crust; set aside. Mix soup,
chicken, vegetables and cheese together; spoon into pie crust. Top
with remaining crust; seal and flute the edges. Cut vents in the top;
bake at 350 degrees for one hour. Serves 4 to 6.

Fresh, green herbs like basil, dill and sage can be rolled
right into a top crust for a pot pie. Lay herbs on the dough and
gently press in with a rolling pin for extra flavor and
an oh-so-pretty appearance.

Enchilada Casserole

Katie French
Portland, TX

*This was one of the first dishes I learned to make as a newlywed.
My husband said he'd like to kiss the person who taught it to me!*

1-1/2 lbs. ground beef,
  browned and drained
14-oz. can enchilada sauce
10-3/4 oz. can cream of
  mushroom soup

10-3/4 oz. can cream of
  chicken soup
10 corn tortillas, torn
8-oz. pkg. shredded
  Cheddar cheese

Combine ground beef, sauce and soups in a large bowl. Stir until well
mixed. In a greased 13"x9" baking pan, layer half of the tortillas, half
of meat mixture and half of the cheese. Repeat layers. Bake, uncovered,
at 350 degrees for 30 minutes. Serves 6 to 8.

Spicy barbecue potato chips make a tasty topping for
Mexican casseroles...just crush 'em up and sprinkle on.

Supper Shortcuts

Green Chile Chicken

Ronni Hall
Springfield, OH

*Pick up a tasty rotisserie chicken from the supermarket
to make this dish in a snap.*

1/2 c. onion, chopped
2 T. butter
3 10-3/4 oz. cans cream of
   mushroom soup
4-oz. can diced pimentos,
   drained

2 4-oz. cans diced green chiles
4 c. cooked chicken, diced
salt and pepper to taste
12-oz. pkg. egg noodles, cooked
2-1/2 to 3 c. shredded sharp
   Cheddar cheese

In a large skillet over medium heat, cook and stir onion in butter until tender. Stir in soup, pimentos and chiles. In a greased 4-quart casserole dish, layer half the noodles and half the chicken; add salt and pepper to taste. Top with half the soup mixture and half the cheese; repeat layers. Bake, uncovered, at 350 degrees for 45 minutes, or until bubbling and cheese is golden. Makes 8 to 10 servings.

Is dinner taking just a little longer than planned? Set out bowls of unshelled walnuts or peanuts for a quick appetizer that will keep tummies from rumbling.

Tena's Delicious Gumbo

Tena Hammond Graham
Evans, GA

This is so easy and so delicious! If you prefer, use the broth that the chicken was cooked in...measure out 6 to 7 cups broth.

4 14-1/2 oz. cans chicken broth
7-oz. pkg. gumbo mix with rice
5 to 6 boneless, skinless chicken
    breasts, cooked and chopped
1 lb. Polish sausage, cut into
    bite-size pieces
2 10-oz. pkgs. frozen
    chopped okra

1 green pepper, chopped
1 red pepper, chopped
1 onion, chopped
pepper to taste
Cajun seasoning to taste
2 14-oz. pkgs. frozen
    popcorn shrimp

Combine all ingredients except shrimp in a large stockpot. Bring to a boil; reduce heat, cover and simmer for 25 minutes. Add shrimp; simmer an additional 5 to 10 minutes. Serves 10 to 12.

Summer's bounty of delicious red and yellow peppers can be saved for winter enjoyment. Fill ice cube trays with diced peppers and water, then freeze. Toss frozen cubes right into simmering dishes for a burst of flavor and color.

Supper Shortcuts

New Orleans Pork Chops

Karen Keilers
Cypress, TX

My sister-in-law served this to us on a visit years ago.
We loved it so much that now I make it at least twice a month!
It's great served with rice or mashed potatoes.

6 pork chops
1 to 2 T. oil
10-3/4 oz. can cream of
   mushroom soup
1/2 c. sour cream

1/2 c. water
1 t. dried parsley, chopped
salt and pepper to taste
2, 8-oz. can French fried onions,
   divided

In a skillet over medium heat, brown pork chops in oil on both sides. Arrange chops in a greased 13"x9" baking pan; set aside. In the same skillet, heat together soup, sour cream, water, seasonings and half the onions. Spread over pork chops. Cover and bake at 350 degrees for one hour. Uncover and top with remaining onions. Return to oven for an additional 5 minutes. Makes 6 servings.

Match background music to the food you're serving for a dinner party that guests will really remember. Check the local library for jazz, salsa or other favorites to set a lively tone...keep it low so everyone can enjoy the conversation.

Smothered Chicken

Sherry Cecil
Wayne, WV

Italian-blend shredded cheese is good in this too.

4 boneless, skinless
   chicken breasts
garlic powder to taste
1 T. oil
4-oz. can sliced mushrooms,
   drained

1 c. shredded Mexican-blend
   cheese
1/2 c. bacon bits
1/2 c. green onion, chopped

Flatten chicken to 1/4-inch thickness; sprinkle with garlic powder.
Heat oil in a large skillet over medium heat; sauté chicken for
4 minutes on each side, until golden. Top chicken with remaining
ingredients. Reduce heat, cover and cook until chicken juices run clear
and cheese is melted. Makes 4 servings.

Swiss Stuffed Chicken

Wanda Minerich
Hibbing, MN

A delicious dish you'll love serving to company.

4 boneless, skinless
   chicken breasts
2 10-3/4 oz. cans cream of
   chicken soup

6 slices Swiss cheese
6-oz. pkg. chicken-flavored
   stuffing mix, prepared

Arrange chicken in a lightly greased 13"x9" baking pan; spread soup
over the top. Arrange cheese slices on top; spread prepared stuffing
over cheese. Cover pan with aluminum foil; bake at 350 degrees for
2 hours, until chicken juices run clear. Serves 4.

Supper Shortcuts

Fiesta Taco Pie

Linda Martindale
El Paso, TX

*My neighbor Lizette made this recipe for me after I came home from
a hospital stay. It tasted so good after that bland hospital food!
Now it's my daughter Andrea's favorite meal.*

8-oz. tube refrigerated
  crescent rolls
1 c. nacho cheese tortilla chips,
  crushed and divided
1 lb. ground beef
1 onion, chopped

8-oz. can tomato sauce
1-1/4 oz. pkg. taco
  seasoning mix
3 T. sour cream
1 c. shredded Cheddar cheese

Separate crescent rolls and line an ungreased 9" pie plate with them;
press together to form a pie crust. Sprinkle with 1/3 cup crushed
tortilla chips and set aside. Brown ground beef and onion in a skillet;
drain. Add tomato sauce and taco seasoning; simmer for 5 minutes.
Pour into pie plate. Spread sour cream over top; sprinkle with cheese
and remaining chips. Bake at 350 degrees for 20 minutes. Makes
6 to 8 servings.

The simplest way to plan a party...choose a theme!
Whether it's Fiesta Night, 1950's Diner or Hawaiian Luau,
a theme suggests appropriate dishes, decorations and music,
and gives guests something fun to look forward to.

Southwest Potato Puff Bake

Monica Taylor
Bluff Dale, TX

A yummy dinner that's also perfect for a game-day brunch.

1/2 lb. ground sausage
1/2 c. green pepper, chopped
1/2 c. onion, chopped
30-oz. pkg. frozen shredded
   hashbrowns, thawed

1 c. shredded Cheddar cheese,
   divided
4 eggs
1/2 c. milk
Garnish: salsa

Brown sausage, pepper and onion together in a skillet over medium heat; drain. Set aside. Layer hashbrowns in a greased 13"x9" baking pan; top with 1/2 cup cheese and sausage mixture. Beat together eggs and milk; pour over the top of sausage. Sprinkle with remaining cheese. Bake at 350 degrees for 30 minutes. Garnish with salsa. Serves 6 to 8.

Dress up stemmed water glasses...tie on a colorful blossom or herb sprig with festive ribbon or raffia.

Supper Shortcuts

Cornbread-Stuffed Roast Chicken

Nancy Wise
Little Rock, AR

Dijon mustard adds a special touch.

2 c. sliced mushrooms
4 T. butter, divided
1-1/2 c. water
4 T. Dijon mustard, divided

1-1/4 t. dried thyme, divided
6-oz. pkg. cornbread
   stuffing mix
3-1/2 lb. chicken

In a skillet over medium heat, sauté mushrooms in 2 tablespoons
butter until tender. Stir in water, 3 tablespoons mustard and
1/4 teaspoon thyme; bring to a boil. Remove from heat; stir in stuffing
mix and spoon loosely into chicken. Place chicken in a roasting pan.
Melt remaining butter in a small saucepan. Stir in remaining mustard
and thyme; brush over chicken. Cover chicken loosely with aluminum
foil and bake for one hour at 375 degrees. Uncover and bake an
additional 30 to 45 minutes, or until juices run clear when pierced.
Let stand for 10 minutes before slicing. Serves 6.

Grab a disposable roasting pan when preparing a big dinner.
Afterwards, just toss it away...no mess to clean up!

Cheese-Stuffed Meatloaf

Belinda Gibson
Amarillo, TX

This recipe freezes great...I like to double it and make 2, serve one tonight and freeze the other for a busy day!

1-1/2 lbs. ground beef
15-oz. can spaghetti sauce,
  divided
2 eggs
1 c. bread crumbs
1/4 c. onion, chopped

1-1/2 T. dried parsley
1 t. salt
1/4 t. pepper
1-1/2 c. shredded mozzarella
  cheese

Combine ground beef, one cup spaghetti sauce and remaining ingredients except cheese. Mix well. Divide meat mixture into thirds; spread one-third in bottom of an ungreased 9"x5" loaf pan. Cover with half the cheese. Repeat layers, ending with meat. Bake at 350 degrees for 30 minutes. Spread meatloaf with reserved sauce; bake for an additional 30 minutes. Serves 4 to 6.

Baking potatoes for the whole family? Stand 'em up in a muffin pan...easy in, easy out of the oven.

Supper Shortcuts

Baked Pork Chops & Potatoes

Phyllis Peters
Three Rivers, MI

*This recipe is a family favorite in the fall
when the weather begins to get cool.*

6 center-cut pork chops
10-3/4 oz. can cream of
   mushroom soup
1 c. sour cream
1 t. dried, minced onion

salt and pepper to taste
2.8-oz. can French fried onions
16-oz. can sliced potatoes,
   drained

Arrange pork chops in a lightly greased 13"x9" baking pan; set aside.
Combine soup, sour cream, minced onion, salt and pepper; spread on
chops. Top with French fried onions. Cover and bake at 325 degrees
for 2 hours, or until chops are tender. Arrange sliced potatoes over
chops; reduce heat to 300 degrees and bake an additional 45 minutes,
until potatoes are warmed through. Makes 6 servings.

Pork chops, chicken breasts and cubed stew beef
brown better if patted dry first with a paper towel.

Easy Chicken-Broccoli Alfredo

Pamela Fasci
Hanson, MA

*The kids love to eat their broccoli when it's served
in a creamy, hearty dish like this one.*

8-oz. pkg. linguine, uncooked
1 c. broccoli flowerets
10-3/4 oz. can cream of
    mushroom soup
1/2 c. milk

1/2 c. grated Parmesan cheese
1/4 t. pepper
2 c. cooked chicken, cubed
Garnish: grated Parmesan
    cheese

Cook half the package of linguine according to package directions, reserving the rest for another recipe. Add broccoli during the last 4 minutes of cooking. Drain; keep warm. Mix soup, milk, cheese and pepper in a saucepan; add chicken. Heat just until bubbly over medium heat; spoon over cooked linguine. Serve with additional Parmesan cheese. Serves 4.

Serve pasta in a warmed serving bowl...a nice touch.
Simply set a colander over the bowl in the sink.
Drain pasta and let stand for a minute, then toss out the
water in the bowl and fill with hot pasta and sauce.

Supper Shortcuts

Ham, Swiss & Asparagus Bake

Lynn Williams
Muncie, IN

*I found this recipe while looking for a way to use up an Easter ham.
It's perfect made with tender spring asparagus, but canned
asparagus is good too.*

1-1/2 c. hot water
6-oz. pkg. chicken-flavored
   stuffing mix
3 c. cooked ham, cubed
18 asparagus spears, cut into
   2-inch pieces

10-3/4 oz. can cream of
   celery soup
1/2 c. milk
1 c. shredded Swiss cheese

Combine water and stuffing mix in a medium bowl; stir just until
moistened. Let stand for 5 minutes. Mix ham, asparagus, soup and
milk in a lightly greased 13"x9" baking pan; sprinkle with cheese.
Top with stuffing. Bake at 350 degrees for 30 minutes, or until heated
through and golden on top. Serves 6.

For buffets or dinner parties, save time by rolling up
flatware in colorful napkins and stacking in a flat basket.
Even kids can help with this well in advance of the
party...one less last-minute task!

Spaghetti Bake

Jill Mehringer
Jasper, IN

My family loves this much better than plain spaghetti...it's cheesy and delicious!

8 to 12-oz. pkg. spaghetti, cooked
2 lbs. ground beef, browned and drained
28-oz. jar spaghetti sauce

4-oz. can sliced mushrooms, drained
3 to 4 c. shredded mozzarella cheese
grated Parmesan cheese to taste

Mix spaghetti, ground beef, sauce and mushrooms together. Spread in a greased 13"x9" baking pan; sprinkle with cheeses. Bake at 350 degrees for 20 minutes, or until cheese is melted. Serves 6.

Chuck Wagon Casserole

Tina Stidam
Delaware, OH

This is easy to prepare the night before...refrigerate overnight, then at dinnertime just whip up the cornbread topping and bake.

1 lb. lean ground beef
1/2 c. onion, chopped
1/2 c. green pepper, chopped
15-1/2 oz. mild chili beans in sauce

3/4 c. barbecue sauce
1/2 t. salt
8-1/2 oz. pkg. corn muffin mix
11-oz. can sweet corn & diced peppers, drained

In a frying pan over medium heat, cook beef, onion and pepper; stir until no longer pink. Drain. Stir in chili beans, barbecue sauce and salt; bring to a boil. Spoon into a lightly greased 13"x9" baking pan and set aside. Prepare corn muffin mix according to package directions; stir in corn and spoon over meat mixture. Bake at 400 degrees for 30 minutes, or until golden. Makes 6 servings.

Supper Shortcuts

Italian Bean & Sausage Pasta

Collette Phillips
Heath, TX

Slice sausage on the diagonal before browning...there's more surface area to get browned.

6-oz. pkg. smoked turkey
  sausage, halved and sliced
14-1/2 oz. can Italian stewed
  tomatoes

14-1/2 oz. can Italian green
  beans, drained
2 c. prepared rotini
1/4 c. grated Parmesan cheese

Cook sausage in a skillet over medium heat until browned. Add tomatoes and beans; bring to a boil for 2 to 3 minutes. Stir in pasta and heat through; sprinkle with cheese. Serves 4.

Paint guests' names on clear glass tealight holders
with acrylic paint. Drop in a tealight candle, then set lit
candles at place settings...a welcoming glow and
a sweet table favor.

Chicken Comfort Casserole

Janie Branstetter
Duncan, OK

Everyone at the next potluck will love it!
Delicious made with leftover turkey too.

7-oz. chicken-flavored rice
   vermicelli mix
4 boneless, skinless chicken
   breasts, cooked and cubed
1/4 c. butter
1/2 c. onion, chopped

1/2 c. green pepper, chopped
1/2 c. celery, chopped
2 10-3/4 oz. cans cream of
   chicken soup
1 c. shredded Cheddar cheese

Prepare rice vermicelli mix according to package directions. Toss with chicken; set aside. Heat butter in a skillet over medium heat; sauté onion, pepper and celery until tender. Combine with rice mixture and soup; spoon into a greased 13"x9" baking pan. Top with cheese; bake at 400 degrees for 20 minutes. Serves 6 to 8.

Flea markets offer an amazing variety of table serving pieces for entertaining! Watch for vintage china, casseroles and jelly-jar glasses to add old-fashioned charm to your dinner table.

Supper Shortcuts

Speedy Beef Stroganoff

Lisa Ludwig
Fort Wayne, IN

Cross-cutting makes the beef tender enough to cook quickly.

1 lb. beef round steak
1/4 c. all-purpose flour
3 T. oil
2/3 c. water
4-oz. can sliced mushrooms

1-1/2 oz. pkg. onion soup mix
1 c. sour cream
cooked egg noodles,
    tossed with butter

Slice meat into thin strips diagonally across the grain; coat with flour. Heat oil in a skillet and brown the beef; drain as needed. Add water, mushrooms and their liquid to skillet; stir in soup mix and heat just to boiling. Blend in sour cream. Serve over buttered noodles. Serves 4.

The easiest-ever way to cook egg noodles...bring water to a rolling boil, then turn off heat. Add noodles and let stand for 20 minutes, stirring twice. Perfect!

Bowtie Pasta & Veggies

Margaret Phares
Jackson Center, PA

This makes a great meal all on its own...sometimes I serve it topped with grilled chicken too. I like to use a colorful frozen chunky vegetable blend like red peppers, broccoli and carrots.

2 T. oil
16-oz. pkg. frozen mixed
   vegetables, thawed
1 yellow squash, diced
1 zucchini, diced
8-oz. pkg. bowtie pasta, cooked
1/4 t. garlic, minced

1/2 t. salt
1/2 c. shredded mozzarella
   cheese
1/2 c. shredded provolone
   cheese
1/2 c. shredded Parmesan
   cheese

Heat oil in a large saucepan over medium heat; sauté vegetables together until lightly golden and tender. Stir in cooked pasta, garlic and salt. Sprinkle with cheeses and stir until melted. Serves 4 to 6.

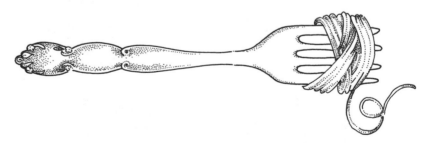

Replace spaghetti sauce in favorite
pasta dishes with mild salsa
for a whole new taste.

Supper Shortcuts

Linguine with Tomato-Clam Sauce

Dianna Likens
Gooseberry Patch

Tomatoes and mushrooms add interest
to white clam sauce over linguine.

2 T. butter
1 T. garlic, minced
1 c. mushrooms, thinly sliced
14-1/2 oz. can chicken broth
2 6-1/2 oz. cans chopped
　clams, drained and 3/4 c.
　liquid reserved
14-1/2 oz. can diced tomatoes,
　drained

1 t. dried parsley
salt and pepper to taste
1/4 c. white wine or
　chicken broth
Optional: 1 T. all-purpose flour,
　1 T. butter, softened
8-oz. pkg. linguine, cooked

Melt butter in a saucepan over medium-high heat. Add garlic and sauté 30 seconds; add mushrooms and sauté one minute. Add broth, clams and reserved liquid, tomatoes, seasonings and wine or broth; bring to a boil and simmer for 5 minutes. If a thicker sauce is desired, whisk flour with softened butter in a small bowl; whisk into sauce, cooking and stirring until thickened. Serve sauce over cooked linguine. Makes 4 to 6 servings.

Feel free to mix & match plates and glasses for a look that's more fun than carefully matched china.

Green Chile Enchiladas

Stephanie Zufelt
Lexington Park, MD

Can't find nacho cheese soup? A can of
medium chili con queso dip will work just as well.

2 lbs. ground beef or turkey,
   browned and drained
2 10-3/4 oz. cans cream of
   chicken soup
10-3/4 oz. can nacho
   cheese soup

4-oz. can diced green chiles
salt and pepper to taste
18 6-inch corn tortillas
16-oz. pkg. shredded
   Colby Jack cheese

Combine browned meat, soups, chiles, salt and pepper. In a lightly
greased 13"x9" baking pan, layer tortillas, meat mixture and cheese,
ending with cheese on top. Bake at 350 degrees until bubbling, about
30 minutes. Serves 6 to 8.

For nifty placecard holders, simply make a small slice in seasonal whole fruits or veggies...apples, peaches, peppers or mini pumpkins. Write guests' names on cards and insert into the slits.

Supper Shortcuts

Tortilla Stew

Donna Cannon
Tulsa, OK

My family absolutely loves this stew, especially in cold weather.
It's ready in less than 40 minutes. Make it with browned
ground beef instead of chicken, if you prefer.

2 10-oz. cans chicken, drained
2 15-1/2 oz. cans hominy
2 15-1/2 oz. cans chili beans
2 14-1/2 oz. cans Mexican-
  style stewed tomatoes
2 11-oz. cans sweet corn &
  diced peppers
2 10-oz. cans tomatoes with
  green chiles

2 1-oz. pkgs. ranch salad
  dressing mix
1/2 onion, chopped
salt and pepper to taste
Garnish: corn or tortilla chips,
  shredded cheese, sour
  cream, guacamole

Stir together all ingredients except garnish in a large stockpot. Simmer over medium heat for 30 minutes. Spoon individual portions over corn or tortilla chips. Garnish as desired with shredded cheese, sour cream and guacamole. Serves 8 to 10.

A simmering stew or chili is so easy to prepare and always welcomed by guests. Pass a basket of warm bread or tortillas, sit back and enjoy your company!

Country Chicken Pot Pie

Vickie

*I like to cut the crust vents with a small
chicken-shaped cookie cutter, just for fun!*

1/4 c. plus 3 T. margarine,
   divided
1-3/4 c. biscuit baking mix,
   divided
1/3 c. plus 2 T. milk, divided

1/4 t. dried parsley
1 c. chicken broth
1 c. frozen mixed vegetables,
   partially thawed
1 c. cooked chicken, cubed

In a mixing bowl, cut 2 tablespoons margarine into one cup baking
mix; stir in 2 tablespoons milk. Pat into the bottom and up the sides of
an ungreased 9" pie plate. Bake at 400 degrees for 5 minutes; set
aside. Melt remaining margarine in a saucepan; stir in 1/4 cup baking
mix and parsley. Heat, stirring constantly, until bubbly; remove from
heat. Stir in chicken broth and vegetables; heat to boiling, stirring
often. Boil for one minute; stir in chicken and heat through. Pour
chicken mixture into crust; set aside. Stir together remaining baking
mix and milk until smooth; spread evenly over chicken mixture. Bake
at 400 degrees until golden, 25 to 30 minutes. Makes 6 to 8 servings.

Fresh fruit makes a colorful garnish for dinner plates.
Try sliced oranges, kiwi or strawberries for a
burst of color that's tasty too.

Supper Shortcuts

Dijon Beef Stew

Amy Butcher
Columbus, GA

*A loaf of crusty French bread, a salad of mixed greens
and steaming bowls of this stew...aah.*

1-1/2 lbs. stew beef, cubed
1/4 c. all-purpose flour
2 T. oil
salt and pepper to taste
2 14-1/2 oz. cans diced
    tomatoes with garlic
    and onion

14-1/2 oz. can beef broth
4 carrots, peeled and cut into
    bite-size pieces
2 potatoes, peeled and cut into
    bite-size pieces
3/4 t. dried thyme
2 T. Dijon mustard

Combine meat and flour in a large plastic zipping bag; toss to coat
evenly. Brown meat in oil over medium-high heat in a stockpot.
Sprinkle to taste with salt and pepper. Add remaining ingredients
except mustard. Bring to a boil; reduce heat. Cover and simmer for
one hour, or until beef is tender. Blend in mustard. Serves 6 to 8.

Talk of joy: there may be things better than beef stew and
baked potatoes and homemade bread...there may be.

–David Grayson

Vinaigrette Beef Kabobs

Tonya Sheppard
Galveston, TX

Cubed chicken thighs are tasty in this recipe too.

3/4 c. vinaigrette salad dressing, divided
1 T. Dijon mustard
1 lb. boneless beef sirloin, cut into 1-inch cubes

8 cherry tomatoes
1 onion, sliced into 8 wedges
1 green pepper, sliced into 8 wedges
4 12-inch wooden skewers

Combine 1/2 cup vinaigrette dressing and mustard in a large plastic zipping bag. Add beef, tomatoes, onion and green pepper; turn to coat. Seal bag and refrigerate for 3 hours or overnight. Remove beef and vegetables from bag, discarding marinade. Thread beef and vegetables alternately onto skewers. Grill or broil kabobs for about 8 minutes, turning occasionally and brushing frequently with remaining dressing, until beef is done and vegetables are tender. Serves 4.

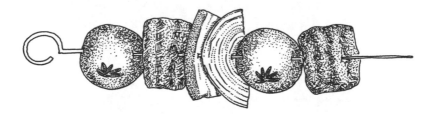

Soak wooden kabob skewers in water at least 20 minutes before using...they won't burn or stick.

Supper Shortcuts

Italian Stuffed Flank Steak

Judy Kantarowski
Marshfield. MA

*I like to arrange the stuffed slices on a platter
with some roasted red potatoes.*

1-lb. beef flank steak
4 slices prosciutto or deli ham
1-1/2 c. roasted red peppers,
   sliced
3/4 c. shredded mozzarella
   cheese

2 cloves garlic, minced
8-oz. pkg. spinach
olive oil
salt and pepper to taste

Pound steak to flatten. Layer prosciutto or deli ham over steak; top
with peppers, cheese, garlic and spinach. Roll up jelly-roll style,
starting with long side; tie with 2 to 3 lengths of kitchen string. Brush
with olive oil and sprinkle with salt and pepper; place in a greased
13"x9" baking pan. Bake, uncovered, at 350 degrees for 40 minutes.
Slice at 2-inch intervals. Serves 4.

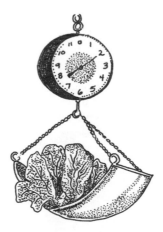

Quickly turn a group of mismatched yard-sale candleholders
into a beautiful set...spray them all with metallic gold or
silver craft paint.

Buttermilk Baked Chicken

Karen Lehmann
New Braunfels, TX

*This chicken makes its own gravy, so be sure to
serve with fluffy mashed potatoes!*

1/4 c. butter
4 boneless, skinless
   chicken breasts
1/2 t. salt
1/2 t. pepper

1-1/2 c. buttermilk, divided
3/4 c. all-purpose flour
10-3/4 oz. can cream of
   mushroom soup

Melt butter in a 13"x9" baking pan in a 425-degree oven; set aside.
Sprinkle chicken with salt and pepper; dip in 1/2 cup buttermilk and
dredge in flour. Arrange chicken in pan; bake at 425 degrees for
25 minutes. Turn chicken over and bake for an additional 10 minutes.
Stir together remaining buttermilk and soup; pour over chicken and
bake for an additional 10 minutes. If necessary, cover with aluminum
foil to prevent browning. Serve chicken drizzled with gravy from dish.
Makes 4 servings.

Twist stems of fresh rosemary around fine wire to
form napkin rings...pleasing to the senses with its
bright green color and spicy scent.

Supper Shortcuts

Zucchini-Stuffed Chicken

Jill Valentine
Jackson, TN

This is a great dish for buffets...sprinkle a little thyme on the chicken before baking for an extra touch of herbal flavor.

2 T. olive oil
2 c. zucchini, shredded
1 onion, finely chopped
6-oz. pkg. herb-flavored
    stuffing mix

3/4 c. water
1 c. shredded Italian-style
    cheese blend
8 chicken leg quarters

Heat oil in a large skillet over medium heat. Add zucchini and onion; cook and stir 5 minutes, or until onion is tender. Remove from heat. Stir in stuffing mix, water and cheese until well blended; cover and set side. Carefully loosen skin on leg quarters to form a pocket; fill evenly with stuffing mixture. Arrange skin-side up in a greased shallow baking pan. Bake at 400 degrees for 45 to 50 minutes, or until chicken juices run clear when pierced. Serves 8.

No peeking! When baking, every time the oven door is opened, the temperature drops 25 degrees.

Garlic Chicken Pizza

Becki Wunderlin
Louisville, KY

Homemade pizza made easy with ready-to-use crusts.

4 T. olive oil
1 lb. boneless, skinless chicken
    breast, cubed
2 cloves garlic, pressed
1/2 t. fresh basil, chopped
1/2 t. fresh rosemary, chopped

2 12-inch Italian pizza crusts
14-oz. jar pizza sauce
16-oz. pkg. shredded mozzarella
    cheese
1 to 2 tomatoes, sliced
Garnish: grated Romano cheese

Heat oil in a large skillet over medium heat. Sauté chicken with garlic
and herbs until chicken juices run clear; set aside. Arrange pizza crusts
on an ungreased baking sheet; brush with olive oil from skillet. Spread
with pizza sauce and chicken mixture; top with mozzarella cheese and
tomato slices. Sprinkle with Romano cheese. Bake at 350 degrees until
cheese bubbles and crusts are firm. Serves 8 to 10.

A sparkling centerpiece...fill a shallow bowl with rock salt,
then nestle in several votive candles.

Supper Shortcuts

Quick Pizza Casserole

Helen Greenstreet
Linthicum, MD

I like to add a layer of sliced pepperoni between the pizza sauce and the cheese...really adds a lot of flavor.

1 lb. ground beef, browned
 and drained
14-oz. jar pizza sauce
8-oz. pkg. shredded
 mozzarella cheese

3/4 c. biscuit baking mix
1-1/2 c. milk
2 eggs

Place beef in an ungreased 8"x8" baking pan; top with pizza sauce and cheese. Combine biscuit mix, milk and eggs in a mixing bowl; stir well until smooth. Pour over cheese; bake at 400 degrees for 30 to 35 minutes. Serves 6.

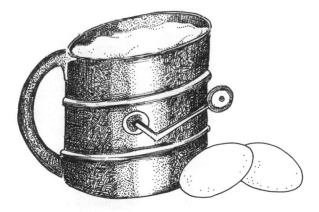

Kids will love mac & cheese or other favorite casseroles
that have been spooned into custard cups for baking.
Easy to serve and just their size!

Quick Kielbasa Skillet

Kristie Rigo
Friedens, PA

This dish only takes about 20 minutes to prepare...perfect for those evenings when dinner needs to be ready in a hurry!

1 lb. Kielbasa, sliced
   1/2-inch thick
1 T. oil
2 15-oz. cans sliced
   potatoes, drained

2 14-1/2 oz. cans French-style
   green beans, drained

Brown Kielbasa in oil in a skillet over medium heat. Add potatoes and beans; cook over low heat until heated through. Serves 4 to 6.

Foods at a dinner party don't have to be fancy...your guests
will be delighted with comfort foods like
Grandma used to make!

Supper Shortcuts

Sweet & Tangy Pork

Cheryl Brady
Canfield, OH

Serve over cooked rice for a complete meal.

1 T. oil
4 boneless pork steaks
10-3/4 oz. can tomato soup
2 T. vinegar
1 T. Worcestershire sauce

1 T. brown sugar
8-oz. can pineapple tidbits,
   drained and 1/4 c. juice
   reserved

Heat oil in a skillet over medium heat. Add steaks and cook until golden on both sides; drain. Stir in soup, vinegar, sauce, brown sugar, pineapple and reserved juice. Cover and simmer over low heat for 5 to 10 minutes until pork is cooked through. Makes 4 servings.

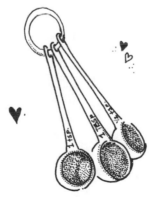

For extra-fluffy white rice, just add a teaspoon
of white vinegar to the cooking water.

Pot Roast in Foil

Maryann Nemecek
Springfield, IL

Great comfort food...I like to put baking potatoes in the oven during the last hour since the roast makes its own gravy.

3 to 4-lb. boneless beef
   chuck roast
1-1/2 oz. pkg. onion soup mix

10-3/4 oz. can cream of
   mushroom soup

Place roast in the center of a length of aluminum foil; sprinkle with soup mix. Pour soup over the top; bring edges of the foil together. Seal well and place in a baking pan. Bake at 350 degrees for 2-1/2 to 3 hours, or until meat is tender. Serves 6 to 8.

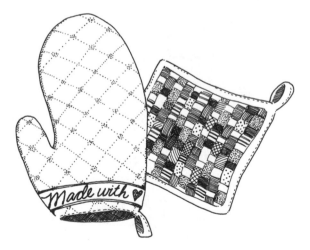

Relax and serve your next dinner party family-style. Guests will enjoy helping themselves from large platters set right on the table. Pass the gravy, please!

Effortless Endings

Rocky Road Brownies

Sheryl Whited
Austin, TX

Add a cup of Spanish peanuts too...yummy!

19-1/2 oz. pkg. fudge
   brownie mix
2 c. mini marshmallows, divided

12-oz. pkg. semi-sweet
   chocolate chips, divided

Prepare brownie mix as directed on package; spread in a greased 13"x9" baking pan. Sprinkle one cup marshmallows and one cup chocolate chips over batter. Bake according to package directions. Remove from oven; sprinkle with remaining marshmallows and chocolate chips. Let cool completely before cutting into squares. Makes 2 to 3 dozen.

Chocolate-Peanut Butter Squares

Rita Brooks
Norman, OK

A really fast, tasty recipe...I use it all the time in a pinch!

18-1/2 oz. chocolate fudge cake
   mix with pudding
1/2 c. oil

2 eggs
6-oz. pkg. peanut butter chips

Mix together dry cake mix, oil and eggs; stir in peanut butter chips. Spread in a greased 13"x9" baking pan. Bake at 350 degrees for 8 minutes. Let cool and cut into 2-inch squares. Makes 3 dozen.

My favorite word is chocolate.
It's the most delicious word I know.

-Maida Heatter

Effortless Endings

Divine Praline Brownies

Sandy Bernards
Valencia, CA

Sugar-coated pecans give brownies a delicious new taste.

22-1/2 oz. pkg. brownie mix
4 T. butter

1 c. brown sugar, packed
1 c. chopped pecans

Prepare brownie mix according to package directions. Spread in a greased 13"x9" baking pan. Set aside. Melt butter in a skillet; add brown sugar and pecans. Heat until sugar dissolves; drizzle over brownie mix. Bake at 350 degrees for 25 to 30 minutes; cut into bars. Keep refrigerated. Makes 12 to 15.

Serve brownie sundaes for an extra-special treat! Place brownies on individual dessert plates and top with a scoop of ice cream, a dollop of whipped topping and a cherry. Yummy!

Raisin Spice Cookies

Deborah Moeller
Thonotosassa, FL

For extra-plump raisins, place them in a small bowl,
pour boiling water over top and let stand for 5 minutes.

18-1/2 oz. pkg. spice cake mix
2 eggs

1/3 c. oil
3/4 c. raisins

Mix all ingredients together; drop by spoonfuls onto ungreased baking sheets. Bake for 12 to 15 minutes at 350 degrees. Let cool for 5 minutes before removing from baking sheets. Makes 1-1/2 dozen.

No time to bake today? Turn store-bought cookies into extra-special delights...melt regular or white chocolate, then dip in half of each cookie. Sprinkle with jimmies or chopped nuts as you like.

Effortless Endings

Mock Lemon Madeleines

Ann Fehr
Trappe, PA

*Substitute lemon extract for the vanilla
if you like extra-lemony cookies.*

8-oz. pkg. cream cheese,
   softened
1/4 c. margarine, softened
1 egg

1 t. vanilla extract
18-1/2 oz. pkg. lemon cake mix
1/2 c. chopped pecans
Garnish: powdered sugar

Blend together cream cheese and margarine; add egg and vanilla.
Stir in dry cake mix and nuts. Drop by teaspoonfuls onto ungreased
baking sheets; flatten slightly. Bake at 350 degrees for 10 to
12 minutes, until bottoms are golden. When cool, sprinkle with
powdered sugar. Makes 1-1/2 to 2 dozen.

Stack cookies, brownies or cupcakes on a
cake stand that's covered with a lace doily or a
vintage tea towel...a pretty presentation in a jiffy!

Chocolate Chip-Cream Cheese Squares
Tiera Lesley
Bartlesville, OK

A chocolatey, creamy delight!

3 8-oz. pkgs. cream cheese,
   softened
1 c. sugar
2-1/2 t. vanilla extract
2 eggs

2 20-oz. tubes refrigerated
   chocolate chip cookie dough,
   divided
12-oz. pkg. semi-sweet
   chocolate chips, melted

Combine cream cheese, sugar, vanilla and eggs; blend until smooth. Press one package cookie dough into the bottom of a greased 13"x9" baking pan. Spread cream cheese mixture over dough; set aside. Slice remaining package of dough 1/2-inch thick. Flatten slices and arrange over cream cheese mixture. Bake for 55 minutes at 350 degrees. Let cool completely. Drizzle with melted chocolate; cut into squares. Makes 2 to 3 dozen.

You can say this for ready-mixes...the next generation
isn't going to have any trouble making pies
exactly like Mother used to make!

-Earl Wilson

184

Effortless Endings

Cookie Cups

Kathy Grashoff
Fort Wayne, IN

*A dollop of whipped cream on top makes these an elegant,
oh-so-easy addition to a dessert tray.*

18-oz. tube refrigerated
    favorite flavor cookie dough

chocolate pudding or
    fruit pie filling

Freeze packaged dough for at least one hour, until firm. Turn a muffin
tin upside-down; spray bottom with non-stick vegetable spray. Slice
frozen dough into 1/2-inch slices; place a slice on the bottom of each
muffin cup. Bake for 11 to 13 minutes at 350 degrees, until dough is
golden and has formed around the cups. Let cool for 5 to 10 minutes;
remove carefully from tin. Fill baked cups as desired with pudding or
pie filling. Makes 16.

Remember that happy feeling as a kid when a party
invitation arrived in the mail? Mail out written invitations
to your next get-together, no matter how informal.
Your grown-up friends will love it!

Chocolate Mint Cookies

Eileen Magiera
Milford, IN

Taste just like everyone's favorite scout cookie! Sometimes I spread a little peanut butter on the crackers before dipping in chocolate.

1 lb. melting chocolate
2 to 3 drops peppermint extract

12-oz. pkg. buttery round
   crackers

Melt chocolate in the top of a double boiler or in a microwave-safe bowl; stir in extract. Dip one cracker at a time into chocolate; place on wax paper until set. Store in plastic freezer bags until serving time. Makes about 8 dozen.

Double Chocolate Bars

Gretchen Hickman
Galva, IL

These are very rich…almost like fudge.

16-oz. pkg. chocolate sandwich
   cookies, crushed
3/4 c. butter, melted
14-oz. can sweetened
   condensed milk

12-oz. pkg. mini chocolate
   chips, divided

Combine cookies and butter; press into an ungreased 13"x9" baking pan. Set aside. Mix condensed milk with one cup of chocolate chips in a microwave-safe bowl. Cover and microwave on high setting until chips are melted, about one minute; stir until smooth. Pour over cookie layer; sprinkle with remaining chips. Bake at 350 degrees for 10 to 12 minutes. Cool; cut into squares. Makes 2 to 3 dozen.

Set up an ice cream buffet! Offer 2 or 3 flavors of ice cream, sweet toppings and a plate of cookies for nibbling. Easy for you, fun for guests!

Effortless Endings

Buckeye Brownies

Heather Prentice
Mars, PA

Chocolate and peanut butter combined...just like buckeye candies.

19-1/2 oz. pkg. brownie mix
2 c. powdered sugar
1/2 c. plus 6 T. butter, softened
   and divided

8-oz. jar creamy peanut butter
6-oz. pkg. semi-sweet
   chocolate chips

Prepare and bake brownie mix in a greased 13"x9" baking pan according to package directions. Let cool. Mix powdered sugar, 1/2 cup butter and peanut butter. Mix well and spread over cooled brownies. Chill for one hour. Melt together chocolate chips and remaining butter in a saucepan over low heat, stirring occasionally. Spread over brownies. Let cool; cut into squares. Makes 2 to 3 dozen.

Make frosted bar cookies look extra-special!
Lightly press a cookie cutter into the frosting, then use
a tube of contrast-color frosting to trace the outline.

Easy Choco-Scotch Cookies

Ann Reimers
Alexandria, MN

Twice the chips...twice the fun!

18-1/4 oz. pkg. yellow cake mix
1/2 c. oil
2 eggs

1 c. semi-sweet chocolate chips
1 c. butterscotch chips

Combine dry cake mix, oil and eggs in a mixing bowl; beat with an electric mixer on medium speed until smooth. Stir in chocolate and butterscotch chips. Drop by teaspoonfuls onto ungreased baking sheets. Bake at 350 degrees for 8 to 10 minutes. Remove to wire racks to cool. Makes 4 to 5 dozen.

Oops! that's the way the cookie (or cake) crumbles!
Turn a mistake into a luscious triumph...simply layer
in a trifle bowl with whipped topping and
sliced strawberries or peaches, then chill.

Effortless Endings

Sugar & Spice Pepper Cookies

Shelby Debus
Fort Pierce, FL

Made with black pepper, these spicy cookies are just a little different!

12-oz. pkg. cinnamon swirl
   quick bread & coffee cake
   mix, divided
1 T. ground ginger
3/4 t. pepper
1/2 t. ground cloves
1/2 c. shortening
1 egg, beaten

Set aside 1/4 cup of swirl mixture from mix. Combine dry quick bread mix, remaining swirl mixture and spices; mix well. Stir in shortening with a fork until mixture looks like coarse crumbs. Add egg; mix well. Shape dough into 1-1/4 inch balls; roll in reserved swirl mixture. Place 2 inches apart on ungreased baking sheets. Bake at 350 degrees for 12 to 14 minutes, or until edges are set. Let cool for one minute before removing from baking sheets. Makes 1-1/2 to 2 dozen.

The simplest centerpiece can be the most festive.
Set 2 or 3 pillar candles on a white plate, then tuck
shiny Christmas balls, seashells or fresh flowers
around the base to highlight the season.

Creamy Key Lime Cheese Pie

Teri Lindquist
Gurnee, IL

*This cool, creamy dessert has been a family favorite for years.
It goes together in a jiffy!*

14-oz. can sweetened
   condensed milk
8-oz. pkg. cream cheese,
   softened
1/2 c. lime juice

1/2 t. vanilla extract
9-inch graham cracker crust
Optional: frozen whipped
   topping, thawed

In a bowl, beat condensed milk, cream cheese and lime juice; blend
until smooth. Stir in vanilla; pour into pie crust. Cover and chill for at
least 3 to 4 hours. Top with whipped topping if desired. Serves 6 to 8.

Need to soften cream cheese in a hurry?
Simply place an unwrapped 8-ounce block on a plate,
and microwave for about a minute at 50% power.

Effortless Endings

Fruit Cocktail Pie

Melodee Book
Denver, PA

Spread with whipped topping, if you like...then decorate with the reserved cherries.

2 c. sour cream
2/3 c. sugar
1 t. vanilla extract

17-oz. can fruit cocktail, drained
9-inch graham cracker crust

Combine sour cream, sugar and vanilla. Remove cherries from fruit cocktail and set aside. Add remaining fruit to mixture. Mix together and pour into crust. Bake at 350 degrees for 20 to 25 minutes. Let cool. Top with cherries for garnish. Keep chilled until ready to serve. Serves 6 to 8.

Make special napkins for your next party...so easy!
Choose paper napkins and stamping ink in coordinating colors,
plus a rubber stamp for the occasion. Lightly stamp
designs onto each napkin.

Peanut Butter-Ice Cream Pie

Jennie Parker
Rochester, NY

My 2 great-grandsons can't get enough of this pie!

1/2 c. whipping cream, whipped
1/2 c. chunky peanut butter
1 qt. vanilla ice cream, softened

9-inch graham cracker crust
1/4 c. graham cracker crumbs

Fold whipped cream and peanut butter into ice cream. Spread in pie crust. Sprinkle with crumbs. Freeze. Makes 6 to 8 servings.

Sticky peanut butter or honey slips right out of a measuring cup if you spray the cup first with non-stick vegetable spray.

Effortless Endings

Favorite Chocolate Pie

Tanya Duke
Bethany, OK

This pie is delicious...so quick & easy to make, yet so elegant.

3.4-oz. pkg. cook & serve
   chocolate pudding mix
2 c. whipping cream, divided
1 c. milk

1/2 c. chocolate chips
9-inch chocolate cookie crust
Garnish: chocolate shavings

Mix together pudding mix, one cup whipping cream, milk and chocolate chips in a saucepan; cook over medium heat, stirring, until thickened. Cool and pour into crust. Chill until set. Whip remaining whipping cream until stiff peaks form; spread over pie. Sprinkle with chocolate shavings. Keep refrigerated. Makes 6 to 8 servings.

Try using refrigerated chocolate chip or sugar cookie dough to make a pie crust for a chilled filling or even for ice cream. Pat dough into pie plate, chill for 30 minutes, then bake as package directs.

Frosty Pineapple Pie

Jo McGruder
Chesterfield, MO

*My mother used to make this pie...it was a must-have
when I started cooking. It's great for a festive luncheon.*

8-oz. can crushed pineapple
3-oz. pkg. lemon gelatin mix
1 c. sugar
1 c. whipping cream

1 T. lemon juice
9-inch graham cracker crust
Garnish: pineapple chunks,
   fresh mint

In a saucepan over medium heat, bring pineapple and its juice to
a boil. Stir in lemon gelatin and sugar until dissolved. Cool just
until almost jelled but still slightly syrupy; set aside. Beat together
whipping cream and lemon juice until stiff peaks form; carefully fold
into pineapple mixture. Pour into pie crust. Chill for several hours or
overnight before serving. Garnish with pineapple chunks and fresh
mint. Serves 6 to 8.

Pop a new powder puff into the flour canister...so handy
for dusting the countertop before rolling out dough
for cookies or pie crust.

Effortless Endings

Cherry Cheese Pie

Cathy Needham
Columbus, OH

This pie is always popular when I take it along to family gatherings!

8-oz. pkg. cream cheese,
   softened
14-oz. can sweetened
   condensed milk

1/4 c. lemon juice
1 t. vanilla extract
9-inch graham cracker crust
21-oz. can cherry pie filling

In a medium bowl, beat cream cheese until light and fluffy. Slowly add condensed milk, beating until smooth. Stir in lemon juice and vanilla until well mixed; pour into crust. Chill for 3 hours, or until firm; top with cherry pie filling. Serves 6 to 8.

Mini Cherry Crescent Pies

Jim Pindell
Hilliard, OH

These are so good we can't wait for 'em to cool!
Sometimes we like to use apple filling...it's delicious too.

8-oz. tube refrigerated
   crescent rolls
12-oz. can cherry pastry filling

2 T. butter, melted
2 to 4 T. sugar
cinnamon to taste

Separate dough into triangles; place on a greased baking sheet. Top each triangle with 2 to 3 teaspoons cherry filling, reserving the rest for another recipe. Roll up each triangle, starting at short end; brush the top of each crescent with butter. Sprinkle with sugar and cinnamon to taste. Bake at 375 degrees for 11 to 13 minutes. Let cool for 5 to 10 minutes. Makes 8.

Line baking sheets with parchment paper
Cut to fit...no sticking and clean-up is easy.

Berry-Pickin' Pie

Diane Goyette
Fairgrove, MI

A perfect pie for summer...tasty made with strawberries too.

3 T. cornstarch
1/2 c. sugar
1-1/2 c. water
3-oz. pkg. raspberry gelatin mix

2 to 3 c. raspberries
9-inch graham cracker crust
Garnish: frozen whipped
   topping, thawed

Combine cornstarch, sugar and water in a saucepan; cook over low heat until thick and bubbly. Remove from heat; gradually add gelatin. Cool; set aside. Place raspberries in pie crust; pour gelatin mixture over top. Refrigerate until set; dollop with whipped topping. Makes 6 to 8 servings.

Roll a tube of chilled cookie dough in chopped pecans or colored sugar before slicing...a quick & easy way to make cookies special.

Effortless Endings

Oh-So-Easy Fruit Tartlets

Jen Licon-Conner
Gooseberry Patch

*Guests will be so impressed with these bakery-style tarts!
Shhh...they're really simple to make. Use your favorite
pudding flavor and fruit to make different varieties.*

2 3.4-oz. pkgs. instant vanilla
   pudding mix
3-1/2 c. milk
2 t. lemon zest
2 4-oz. pkgs. mini graham
   cracker crusts

Garnish: sliced kiwi, peaches
   or strawberries, mandarin
   oranges, raspberries,
   blueberries
1/2 c. apple jelly, melted

Prepare pudding according to package directions, using the milk. Stir
in lemon zest. Spoon into mini crusts; arrange fruit on top as desired.
Use a pastry brush to glaze fruit with melted jelly. Set tartlets on a
baking sheet, cover and chill. Makes one dozen.

Make guests feel like kids again with charming
candy napkin rings! Wrap candy necklaces around
rolled napkins or cut paper strips of candy dots
to fit around napkins and join the ends with tape.

Peaches & Cream Dessert

Rebecca Roth
Hurley, SD

Just peachy...a potluck favorite.

18-1/2 oz. pkg. yellow cake mix
1/2 c. butter, softened
14-1/2 oz. can peach pie filling
15-oz. can sliced peaches,
    drained

1/2 c. sugar
1 t. cinnamon
1 c. sour cream
1 egg, beaten

Combine cake mix with butter until crumbly; pat into an ungreased
13"x9" baking pan. Spread pie filling over the top; lay peaches on
pie filling. Set aside. Mix sugar and cinnamon; sprinkle over peaches.
Blend sour cream and egg together; spread over sugar mixture.
Bake at 350 degrees for 25 to 35 minutes, until edges are golden.
Serves 8 to 10.

Substitute margarine for butter when baking, if you like.
Don't substitute reduced-fat spreads, though...they contain
more water than butter or margarine and will not give
the same baking results.

Effortless Endings

Fluffy Chocolate-Peanut Butter Pie

Jennie Gist
Gooseberry Patch

This tasty pie takes about 5 minutes to prepare...it's just as delicious made with sugar-free or fat-free products.

2 c. milk
2 3.9-oz. pkgs. instant
   chocolate pudding mix
1/2 c. creamy peanut butter
9-inch graham cracker crust

8-oz. container frozen whipped
   topping, thawed
Optional: semi-sweet mini
   chocolate chips

Combine milk and pudding mix in a medium bowl. Whisk together until thickened; stir in peanut butter. Spoon into crust; spread with whipped topping. If desired, garnish with mini chocolate chips. Chill for several hours until firm. Serves 6 to 8.

Garnish a special dessert with chocolate cut-outs!
Spread melted chocolate thinly on wax paper
and chill until nearly set. Cut out hearts or flowers
with cookie cutters, chill again, then gently peel off.
Arrange on top of a cake or even stand upright
in a drift of whipped topping. Aren't you clever!

Millionaire Pie

Linda Bremkamp
Palatka, FL

This pie is so light and delicious!

8-oz. pkg. cream cheese,
   softened
1/4 c. milk
20-oz. can crushed pineapple
1 c. chopped pecans

1-oz. pkg. instant white
   chocolate pudding mix
8-oz. container frozen whipped
   topping, thawed
2 9-inch graham cracker crusts

In a large bowl, beat cream cheese and milk with an electric mixer on medium speed until smooth. Add pineapple and its juice, pecans and pudding mix; blend well with a spoon. Fold in whipped topping. Spoon into pie crusts; chill for 30 minutes, or until ready to serve. Makes 2 pies; each pie serves 6 to 8.

Cookies made from chilled dough can be stamped with
items found around the kitchen. Slice dough and lightly press
an object into the top...a meat tenderizer, a pasta die
or even the bottom of a juice glass, then bake as usual.

Effortless Endings

Strawberry-Yogurt Pie

Janice Ruckelshausen
Sheldon, IA

Try strawberry-flavored whipped topping for a triple berry delight!

8-oz. container frozen whipped
 topping, thawed
8-oz. container strawberry
 yogurt

10-oz. pkg. frozen strawberries,
 thawed
9-inch graham cracker crust

Mix whipped topping, yogurt and strawberries together; spoon into pie crust. Refrigerate. Serves 6 to 8.

Make your own colored sugar...easy! Place a cup of sugar
in a plastic zipping bag, then add 2 or 3 drops of food coloring.
Knead the bag until color is mixed throughout, then spread
sugar on a baking sheet to dry.

Oklahoma Coconut Cake

Sandra Vance
Galena, OH

Creamy, rich and gooey through and through.

18-1/2 oz. pkg. yellow cake mix
14-oz. can sweetened
   condensed milk
8-oz. can cream of coconut

8-oz. container frozen whipped
   topping, thawed
1 c. sweetened flaked coconut
1/2 c. chopped pecans

Bake cake in a greased 13"x9" baking pan according to package directions. While cake is still hot, poke holes in the top with a fork; set aside. Mix together condensed milk and cream of coconut; pour over cake. When cake has cooled completely, spread with whipped topping; sprinkle with coconut and pecans. Keep refrigerated. Makes 8 to 10 servings.

Substitute pineapple, apple or orange juice for water in packaged cake mixes for extra flavor.

Effortless Endings

Caramel Apple Cake

Sherry Morris
Sandwich, IL

*A perfect fall dessert...try a tart baking apple
like Gala or Granny Smith.*

1-1/2 c. biscuit baking mix
2/3 c. sugar
1/2 c. milk
2 c. apples, cored, peeled
    and sliced

1 T. lemon juice
3/4 c. brown sugar, packed
1/4 t. cinnamon
1 c. boiling water

Combine baking mix and sugar; stir in milk. Pour into a greased
9"x9" baking pan; top with apples. Sprinkle with lemon juice; set
aside. Mix brown sugar and cinnamon; sprinkle over apples. Pour
water over the top; bake at 350 degrees for 50 minutes to one hour.
Serve with Sweetened Whipped Cream. Serves 4 to 6.

Sweetened Whipped Cream:

3/4 c. whipping cream

2 T. sugar

Blend cream and sugar together in a chilled bowl. Beat with an
electric mixer on high speed until stiff peaks form.

Need a cake stand for your special creation?
Set a plate on an inverted bowl.

Banana-Nut Pudding Cake

*Margaret Revis
Sherrills Ford, NC*

A banana lover's dream!

18-1/4 oz. pkg. banana-walnut
   snacking cake mix
3 bananas, sliced
3-1/2 oz. pkg. instant banana
   pudding mix
2 c. milk

8-oz. pkg. cream cheese,
   softened
8-oz. container frozen whipped
   topping, thawed
1/2 c. chopped walnuts

Prepare cake mix according to package directions; pour into a greased 13"x9" baking pan. Bake at 350 degrees for 15 to 20 minutes; let cool. Top with bananas; set aside. Beat pudding mix, milk and cream cheese with an electric mixer until smooth; spread over bananas. Spread whipped topping over pudding; sprinkle with walnuts. Chill. Serves 8 to 10.

Create a pretty marbleized effect when baking a white cake mix. Simply sprinkle batter in its pan with a few drops of food coloring, then swirl the color around with a knife tip.

Effortless Endings

Chocolate-Cherry Cake

Renee Redcloud
Nashville, TN

This is a delicious cake, especially for potlucks.
Bake it in a disposable pan so you can leave the leftovers
at the party...if there ARE any leftovers!

18-1/2 oz. pkg. devil's food
   cake mix
21-oz. can cherry pie filling
2 eggs
1 T. almond extract

1 c. sugar
5 T. butter
1/2 c. evaporated milk
1 c. milk chocolate chips
1 t. vanilla extract

Combine cake mix, pie filling, eggs and extract in a mixing bowl.
Beat with an electric mixer on high speed until well mixed (cherries
will break up somewhat). Pour into a greased 13"x9" baking pan and
bake according to package directions. About 5 minutes before cake is
done, whisk together sugar, butter and evaporated milk in a saucepan
over medium heat. Bring to a boil; boil for one minute. Remove
saucepan from heat and stir in chocolate chips and vanilla. Remove
cake from oven; immediately pour icing over cake. Let cake stand for
at least one hour. Serves 8 to 10.

Toast nuts for extra flavor. Place a single layer of walnuts,
pecans or almonds in a skillet. Stir or shake skillet over
medium-high heat continually for 5 to 7 minutes. Nuts are
done when they start to turn golden and smell toasty.

Orange Dream Cake

Patti Manion
Mechanicsburg, PA

This cake tastes just like our favorite orange and cream frozen pop.

18-1/4 oz. pkg. orange cake mix
3-oz. pkg. orange gelatin mix
1/2 c. boiling water
1/2 c. cold water
3-1/2 oz. pkg. instant vanilla
   pudding mix

2 t. vanilla extract
1 c. milk
1 t. orange extract
8-oz. container frozen whipped
   topping, thawed

Prepare cake mix according to package directions; bake in a greased 13"x9" baking pan. Dissolve gelatin in boiling water; add cold water. Use a fork to poke cake full of holes; slowly pour gelatin over cake. Refrigerate for one hour. In a medium bowl, whisk together pudding mix, vanilla extract, milk and orange extract. Fold in whipped topping; spread over cake. Store in refrigerator. Serves 8 to 10.

To make a cake extra rich, substitute 2 egg yolks
for each whole egg.

Effortless Endings

Piña Colada Cake

Debra Eaton
Mesa, AZ

*A cool and refreshing dessert...best made
the same day it's served so it doesn't get soggy.*

18-1/2 oz. pkg. yellow cake mix
15-oz. can cream of coconut
8-oz. can crushed pineapple,
  drained

2 c. frozen whipped topping,
  thawed
2 T. sweetened flaked coconut,
  toasted

Prepare cake mix according to package directions; bake in a greased
13"x9" baking pan. When cake has cooled, use a fork to poke holes
in the top. Spread cream of coconut evenly over top of cake. Sprinkle
with pineapple; spread whipped topping over entire surface. Sprinkle
with coconut; chill. Makes 8 to 10 servings.

Scoop portions of Piña Colada Cake into stemmed glasses
and top with a dollop of whipped cream and
a paper umbrella, just for fun!

Fast Fruit & Cake Dessert

Jeannie Agentis
Coopersburg, PA

So easy a child can make it...so tasty there's never any left!

1/4 c. oil
18-1/4 oz. pkg. yellow cake mix
2 eggs

1/2 c. water
21-oz. can cherry or blueberry
 pie filling

Pour oil into a 13"x9" baking pan; tilt to coat the bottom. Pour cake mix, eggs and water into pan. Stir with a fork until well blended, about 2 minutes. Spoon pie filling over batter and bake for 35 to 45 minutes. Serves 8 to 10.

A long skewer or even a strand of spaghetti is useful in testing the doneness of deep cakes.

Effortless Endings

Sweet Hummingbird Cake

Wendy Lee Paffenroth
Pine Island, NY

A sprinkle of chopped pecans makes a nice finish to this rich cake.

8-oz. can crushed pineapple
2 to 3 bananas, sliced
1/2 c. milk
2 eggs
1/4 c. oil

1 t. vanilla extract
Optional: 1/4 c. dark rum
18-1/2 oz. pkg. banana
   cake mix
16-oz. can vanilla frosting

Beat together pineapple with juice, bananas, milk, eggs, oil, vanilla extract and rum, if using, until well blended. Stir in cake mix until moistened. Pour into a greased and floured Bundt® cake pan. Bake at 350 degrees on middle oven rack for 40 minutes, until top springs back when touched. Cool for at least 45 minutes; invert onto a serving plate. Microwave frosting on high setting 15 to 20 seconds, until runny. Let stand for a minute before drizzling over cake. Serves 12.

For easy-to-make frosting that's not too sweet,
simply blend together a 16-ounce can of frosting with an
8-ounce package of softened cream cheese.

Pecan Pie Cake

Sue Hart
Mena, AR

So yummy I could eat it all by myself!

18-1/2 oz. pkg. yellow cake
   mix, divided
1/2 c. margarine, melted
4 eggs, divided
1-1/2 c. light corn syrup

1/2 c. brown sugar, packed
1 t. vanilla extract
1/8 t. salt
1-1/2 c. chopped pecans

Set aside 2/3 cup of cake mix for topping. Combine remaining cake mix with melted margarine and one egg; mix well. Press into a greased and floured 13"x9" baking pan; bake at 350 degrees for 20 minutes. Mix reserved cake mix, remaining eggs, corn syrup, brown sugar, vanilla and salt. Pour over baked cake; sprinkle with pecans. Bake for an additional 30 minutes at 350 degrees. Let cool. Serves 8 to 10.

Chopped or crushed candy bars make a fast & easy topping for frosted cakes. Try using toffee, caramel or nougat bars...mmm!

Effortless Endings

Triple Chocolate Cake

Jane Harm
Neenah, WI

A chocolate lover's delight.

18-1/4 oz. pkg. devil's food
   cake mix
4-1/2 oz. pkg. instant chocolate
   pudding mix
1-3/4 c. milk

12-oz. pkg. semi-sweet
   chocolate chips
2 eggs
Garnish: powdered sugar

Combine cake mix, pudding mix, milk, chocolate chips and eggs in a large bowl. Mix by hand until well blended, about 2 minutes. Pour batter into a greased and floured Bundt® pan. Bake at 350 degrees for 50 to 55 minutes, or until cake springs back when touched. Do not overbake. Turn out onto a serving plate; sift powdered sugar on top before serving. Serves 10 to 12.

Cover the tube in a Bundt® pan with a small paper cup...when you pour in the batter, it won't spill down the center hole.

Coconut Crown Pound Cake

Doris Tschoerner
Austin, TX

This cake will be the crowning glory of your dessert table!

18-1/2 oz. pkg. French vanilla
    cake mix
3-1/4 oz. pkg. instant vanilla
    pudding mix
4 eggs

1 c. sour cream
1/2 c. oil
2 t. coconut extract
1/2 c. sweetened flaked coconut

Combine cake mix, pudding mix, eggs, sour cream, oil and extract; beat for 2 minutes with an electric mixer on medium speed. Stir in coconut; pour into a greased and floured Bundt® cake pan. Bake at 350 degrees for 45 to 50 minutes. Let cool in pan; invert onto a serving plate. Spread Coconut Icing over the top. Serves 10 to 12.

Coconut Icing:

16-oz. can cream
    cheese frosting

2 t. coconut extract
1/2 c. sweetened flaked coconut

Mix all ingredients together until smooth.

For a decorative finish on a frosted cake, create wavy lines
by drawing the tines of a fork through the frosting.

Effortless Endings

Chocolate Chip Cake

Sandy McGraw
Abilene, TX

For an extra-special touch, drizzle melted chocolate over cake.

18-1/4 oz. pkg. yellow cake mix
3-1/2 oz. pkg. instant chocolate
   pudding mix
8-oz. container sour cream
1/2 c. oil

1/2 c. water
4 eggs
12-oz. pkg. semi-sweet mini
   chocolate chips
Garnish: powdered sugar

Combine all ingredients except chocolate chips and powdered sugar. Beat well. Add chocolate chips and stir. Pour into a greased and floured Bundt® pan. Bake at 350 degrees for one hour. When cake has cooled, invert onto a serving plate; sprinkle with powdered sugar. Serves 10 to 12.

Serving ice cream is a snap...place scoops in a paper-lined muffin tin and freeze. At dessert time, each scoop will be all ready to top pie à la mode or place beside slices of cake.

The Queen's Strawberry Cake

Wendy Lee Paffenroth
Pine Island, NY

A cake fit for a queen! Serve with
French vanilla ice cream or whipped cream.

10-oz. pkg. frozen strawberries,
   thawed
18-1/4 oz. pkg. white cake mix
1/2 c. water

1/2 c. oil
4 eggs
3-oz. pkg. strawberry
   gelatin mix

Drain strawberries; reserve 1/3 cup juice and set aside. Combine cake mix, water and oil in a mixing bowl; beat until smooth. Add eggs, one at a time, beating after each addition. Add half of the strawberries and reserved juice. Add gelatin and blend all together. Pour into a greased 13"x9" pan; spoon remaining strawberries on top. Bake at 350 degrees for 30 to 40 minutes. Let cool; invert onto serving plate. Serves 8 to 10.

Sprinkle powdered sugar or cocoa through a doily for
a pretty yet simple cake decoration...check craft stores
for holiday stencils too!

Effortless Endings

Mandarin Orange Cake

Nancy Likens
Wooster, OH

*This is my daughter's favorite cake! She asks for it on her birthday,
at Christmas, on New Year's Day...and now she makes it herself
whenever the opportunity arises!*

18-1/2 oz. pkg. white cake mix
11-oz. can mandarin oranges,
   drained and juice reserved
3 egg whites
1/2 c. oil
Garnish: 1/2 c. sweetened
   flaked coconut

Combine cake mix, reserved orange juice, egg whites and oil. Blend
with an electric mixer on medium speed for 2 minutes, until creamy.
Fold in oranges; pour into a greased and floured 13"x9" baking pan.
Bake at 350 degrees for 25 to 35 minutes, until a toothpick inserted
in the center comes out clean. Cool in pan for 10 minutes; remove to
a wire rack to cool completely. Transfer to a serving platter. Frost top
and sides with Pineapple Topping; sprinkle with coconut. Serves 12.

Pineapple Topping:

2 8-oz. cans crushed pineapple
3-1/2 oz. pkg. instant vanilla
   pudding mix
8-oz. container frozen whipped
   topping, thawed
1/2 c. sweetened flaked coconut

Pour pineapple and its juice in a medium mixing bowl; stir in pudding
mix and fold in whipped topping and coconut. Mix well and chill
while cake is cooling.

*Crush nuts quickly...place them in a plastic zipping bag
and roll over them with a rolling pin. No rolling pin?
Use a heavy food can.*

Kitchen ♥ Basics

Measure ingredients...

liquids - use a glass measuring cup, fill to the marked line

solids - use a plastic or metal measuring cup or spoon, fill to the top and level off with a knife

Chip Chop...

Chop - cut up, not too finely

Mince - cut up very finely

Cube - cut into cubes, 1/2 inch or larger

Dice - cut into small cubes, 1/2 inch or less

Sauté...

cook and stir in oil in a skillet over medium heat

Kitchen ♥ Basics

Simmer...
bring to a boil, lower heat and cook slowly just below the boiling point

Bake...
preheat the oven for 5 to 10 minutes before putting the pan into it

Test for doneness...
insert a wooden pick into the center of a cake...if it's dry when removed, the cake is done

Chill...
place in the refrigerator (not the freezer) until chilled through

Easy Entertaining

☑ Party Checklist

3 weeks before...
- ☐ Choose party theme and date
- ☐ Make guest list
- ☐ Send out invitations requesting RSVP's within 2 weeks
- ☐ Plan menu and shopping list
- ☐ Ask a friend to help as needed

1 to 2 weeks before...
- ☐ Buy, make or borrow decorations, serving pieces and table settings
- ☐ Shop for all (except last-minute) groceries
- ☐ Prepare and freeze any foods that can be made in advance

A few days before...
- ☐ Call any guests who haven't responded yet
- ☐ Clean out fridge to make room for party foods

The day before...
- ☐ Shop for last-minute foods, fresh flowers and ice
- ☐ Do any last-minute cleaning
- ☐ Set up tables, chairs, decorations, etc.
- ☐ Thaw frozen party foods

The day of the party...
- ☐ Prepare or pick up last-minute foods
- ☐ Set out foods and beverages
- ☐ Take time for yourself to relax and get dressed
- ☐ Turn on party music
- ☐ Greet guests and have a wonderful time!

After the party...
- ☐ Jot down a few notes...a big help for next party! What foods were most popular? Was there too much or not enough of anything? What else did people especially like?

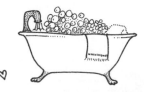

You're Invited!

When: _____

Where: _____

What to bring: _____
_____
_____

Please reply to: _____
_____

Copy, Color & Cut Out!

Here's a ready-to-use invitation for your next get-together with friends & family.

Use this table tent to tell everyone what goodies are being served!

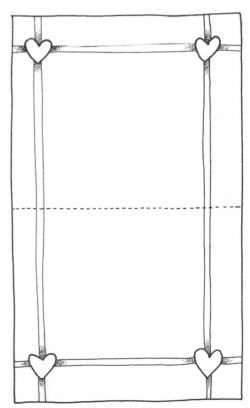

Index

Appetizers

Breads

Breakfast

Desserts

Index

Mains

Salads

Index

Sides

Soups

We've cooked up a whole collection of Gooseberry Patch® books!

Have a taste for more? Call us toll-free at
1-800-854-6673
We'll send you our latest catalog filled with kitchenware, candles, handmade quilts, gourmet goodies, enamelware, bowls, bubble night lights and our very own line of cookbooks, calendars and organizers!

Phone us:
1·800·854·6673

Fax us:
1·740·363·7225

Visit our website:
www.gooseberrypatch.com

Send us your favorite recipe!

and the memory that makes it special for you!* If we select your recipe for a brand new **Gooseberry Patch** cookbook, your name will appear right along with it...and you'll receive a FREE copy of the book! Mail to:

Vickie & Jo Ann
Gooseberry Patch, Dept. Book
600 London Road
Delaware, Ohio 43015

*Please include the number of servings and all other necessary information!

make it easy • carefree cooking • it's a snap • old-fashioned goodness ... for today!

(only easier) • piping hot • came & get it! • make it easy • carefree cooking • delicious dinners • just like Mom's

U.S. to Canadian recipe equivalents

Volume Measurements

1/4 teaspoon	1 mL
1/2 teaspoon	2 mL
1 teaspoon	5 mL
1 tablespoon = 3 teaspoons	15 mL
2 tablespoons = 1 fluid ounce	30 mL
1/4 cup	60 mL
1/3 cup	75 mL
1/2 cup = 4 fluid ounces	125 mL
1 cup = 8 fluid ounces	250 mL
2 cups = 1 pint =16 fluid ounces	500 mL
4 cups = 1 quart	1 L

Weights

1 ounce	30 g
4 ounces	120 g
8 ounces	225 g
16 ounces = 1 pound	450 g

Oven Temperatures

300° F	150° C
325° F	160° C
350° F	180° C
375° F	190° C
400° F	200° C
450° F	230° C

Baking Pan Sizes

Square

8x8x2 inches	2 L = 20x20x5 cm
9x9x2 inches	2.5 L = 23x23x5 cm

Rectangular

13x9x2 inches	3.5 L = 33x23x5 cm

Loaf

9x5x3 inches	2 L = 23x13x7 cm

Round

8x1-1/2 inches	1.2 L = 20x4 cm
9x1-1/2 inches	1.5 L = 23x4 cm